MY HAIR IS STILL PROFESSIONAL TOO!: WHERE ARE WE NOW?

April Maria Williams

Jumptime Publishing

Copyright © 2022 April Maria Williams

All rights reserved

No part of this book may be reproduced, or stored in a retrieval system, or transmitted in any form or by any means, electronic, mechanical, photocopying, recording, or otherwise, without express written permission of the publisher.

ISBN-13: 978-1737859574

*This book is dedicated to my favorite lady,
My Mom! Love you lady!*

Table Of Contents

1. Introduction
2. What's Going On With The Crown Act And Why Is It Stalled?
3. What's In Those Products That Black People Use In Their Hair?
4. Now: Real World Recent Hair Stories Of Discrimination In The Workplace
5. Respectability Politics: Making Our Plight Harder?
6. Now: Real World Stories Of Hair Discrimination In Schools
7. Hair Discrimination Is Not Just An American Issue, But A Global Concern
8. Black Hair On Display
9. What Do We Do Now To End Hair Discrimination?

Citations

APRIL MARIA WILLIAMS

Introduction

Over the last few years, a spotlight has been placed on Black hair and natural hairstyles worn by Black people of all ages. There is an ongoing trend of Black women, men, and children being discriminated against for embracing their natural hair textures and hairstyles akin to African culture. For many years Black people have worn the hairstyles that allowed us to fit into what society deems acceptable, ignoring the plight that Black people may face when forced to conform to societal standards. No one should have to deal with hair discrimination because hair can come in many colors, textures, and styles. Legislation needs to be passed and enforced in the United States and globally to ensure that Black women, men, and children are no longer forced to wear certain hairstyles for fear of hair discrimination. Society needs to get to the place where we look at hair as being just hair.

The physical appearance of an attorney matters. An attorney needs to be taken seriously. Attorneys want the best outcomes for the clients they serve. As a Black female attorney, conforming to societal standards of professionalism in my career field is difficult. Especially when trying to maintain my natural hair look and stay in line with the professional standards that have been set by society for Black women. There are always constant decisions about how best to style my hair. Should I wear my hair picked out into an afro or in its natural state? Should I wear it in a bun pulled back, braids, or twists. Should I just wear it straight or in a relaxed style? While each one of these hairstyles are beautiful, having to decide which one is appropriate to fit into society should not be at the forefront of grooming decisions for Black women. Particularly when the hairstyle has no bearing on your abilities or capabilities as to what you are doing in the present moment. Far too often, a personal preference takes precedence in the decisions and perceptions of another person. The personal preferences are, in many cases, those that mimic one group of people, usually White or European standards, that have been established to be the norm at the exclusivity of the differences that other races may have.

There is the judgment that Black people deal with when societal standards are not met. People who are not subjected to these standards may not realize how detrimental these standards and statements are to Black members of society. But we are all programmed to maintain and uphold the standards. For example, there is always a great debate every time a Black woman changes her hair. I remember the first time I wore my hair in an afro with a hairpin on the side at the first big law firm I worked for. A white colleague walked up to me and said, "Oh wow, I have never seen your hair out; it's so big." I was excited about my hair being out for the first time, but I did not expect that comment. Being accustomed to comments like that, I responded, "Yes, isn't it great?" Your hair is "big" is a normal comment that I receive from White people when I wear my natural hair in an afro. I would like to believe that they are just unaware of how troubling the comment is. Calling a Black person's hair big suggests that it is not normal, that something is wrong with it, and that it does not belong in the current setting. A Black person's natural afro is just hair, and while a different density, it is not lacking or needing opinions; it just needs the recognition and acceptance of being hair.

My first time in court as an attorney was comforting, however. The judge was a black woman who wore an afro herself. The county where I practice was the first county to have elected a large number of Black women to the bench.[i] It was comforting to see someone that looked like me my first time out. I wore my hair in a front braid with a little hair out in the back. The judge was very nice. Afterwards, even though I did not get to speak while court was in session, the judge asked me to come introduce myself and complemented me on my hairstyle. I realized after the fact, that I may not have had the same experience if I was in another court room. While the county where I live is more liberal, there is still a decorum and ceiling that needs to be broken when it comes to a Black woman's hair. Maybe no one would have cared about my hair or maybe implicit bias would have shown its face, but I am just glad that my first time in a Texas court as an attorney happened in this manner. It was fuel for me to keep going and pushing to end discrimination and specifically, hair discrimination.

Where are we now as it pertains to the laws that protect hairstyles that are akin to African culture? Since My Hair Is Professional TOO! was released, The CROWN Act has been introduced in numerous states, passing in just 19 states.[ii] There has been increased awareness around ending hair discrimination against Black people, and stories about occurrences of hair discrimination whether in school, work, and socially. In many cases these stories have made local and national headlines, as well as multiple views on social media platforms. Across working professions, as more and more Black people enter higher ranking positions, discussions about hair discrimination are being had in the open. But most states legislatures and many in the United States Congress are wholly unwilling to advance this type of legislation.

In my book My Hair Is Professional TOO!, we discussed the history of the laws that make it legal for an employer to discriminate based on how you choose to style your hair.[iii] Particularly outlining the case laws that have shaped these types of discrimination. We identified that the use of gender discrimination case rulings was used as the framework for what later shaped court's opinions on hair discrimination cases.

We learned that an immutable verses mutable standard was used then and continues to be used now.[iv] Immutable traits were identified as those traits that cannot be changed about a person. They are traits that are passed down biologically from a parent to child such as a person's race. Immutable traits are protected under the constitution because it is a trait that cannot be changed. Mutable traits are those that can be changed without great difficulty, such as the length of a person's hair. The courts have reasoned that because a person's hairstyle can be "easily changed", it does not rise to the level of protection that other immutable traits have protection under.[v] The book argues that because some Black people have denser hair, they need other types of hairstyles to maintain and protect their hair.[vi] No one should be discriminated against when they choose to wear hairstyles to protect their hair. The book also argues that Black hairstyles are a part of a Black person's culture, which is a part of a person's race, and thus it should be protected under the law.[vii]

In My Hair Is Professional TOO!, we also learn that disparate treatment and disparate impact are two distinct concepts that cannot be interchanged. Proving a disparate treatment claim involves showing that there was intentional discrimination.[viii] This means that a member of a protected class is denied the same employment opportunities that are available to other employees.[ix] Proving a disparate impact claim involves showing that an employer's policies or practices have an adverse impact on a person that is a member of a protected class.[x] In disparate impact claims, employers usually refuse to change their policies after finding out that the policy has a particular impact on a protected class.[xi] In the leading case on hair discrimination,

EEOC v. Catastrophe Management, the court specifically disallowed showing that there was disparate treatment to assert a disparate impact claim.[xii]

In EEOC v. Catastrophe Management, the court upheld the ruling that an employer can discriminate based on how a person chooses to wear their hair.[xiii] In that case, the employer told a potential employment candidate that she could not wear her locs at work because according to the hiring manager, "they tend to get messy."[xiv] It was argued in that case, that having a policy that discriminates based on a cultural hairstyle worn by a particular race, is race based discrimination.[xv]

The court disagreed with that argument. In a rehearing, the Justices' that reviewed the case sided with Catastrophe Management and believed that a legitimate argument was not made.[xvi] The court struck down the EEOC's claims citing that the hairstyles were mutable and thus can be changed easily.[xvii] As mentioned previously, if something is mutable, there is no need for protections under the law. The dissent in the rehearing strongly disagreed.[xviii] Justice Martin, the dissenting judge in this case, felt that the majority used pseudoscience to conclude that Black hair did not need protection under the law.[xix] With the hopes of prevailing on the side of rightness, to our dismay, the case was denied at the highest level.[xx] The Supreme Court of the United States refused to hear the case. This leaves America with a federal ruling that allows an employer to discriminate against an employee based on how they style their hair.[xxi] State and federal legislatures are now tasked with the duty to prevent this type of discrimination.

Without federal, state, or local intervention, Black men, women, and children are left to conform to the standards that have been set by the majority. Standards that were set to be exclusive, but not necessarily inclusive to all members of society. Black men and women are still being told to change their hair to work with employers. It has been revealed that these standards are not only being used in the workplace, but they are finding their way into our kid's schools and extracurricular activities. These standards are being weaponized. The idea that a person's hair in its natural state, as it naturally grows from one's head[xxii] can cause this much discussion and controversy is taboo. However, history continues to reinforce that we live in a white dominated society, that seeks to maintain their standards in almost every aspect of life. As this book will reveal, it is time for hair discrimination to end. It is time for the Crown Act to be passed and enforced. Not just in the United States but across the globe.

What's Going On With The CROWN Act And Why Is It Stalled?

In December of 2019, the Creating a Respectful and Open World for Natural Hair bill aka the CROWN Act was introduced to the House of Representatives by Representative Cedric Richmond of Louisiana.[xxiii] The CROWN Act makes it illegal to discriminate based on hair styles that are associated with racial minorities.[xxiv] "The bill specifically names several hairstyles more commonly associated with Black people, including afros, bantu knots, braids, cornrows, dreadlocks, and twists."[xxv] The legislation gained a lot of traction when it was introduced federally as more states began to pass their own versions of the bill, but ultimately the bill failed to move forward in the Senate after being introduced by New Jersey Senator Corey Booker.[xxvi] In March of 2022, the act was introduced again by Representative Bonnie Watson Coleman of New Jersey. The bill passed through the House of Representatives but has yet to receive a vote in the senate.[xxvii]

As of the fall of 2022, the CROWN Act has passed in 19 states including:

California, New York, New Jersey, Virginia, Colorado, Washington, Maryland, Connecticut, New Mexico, Delaware, Nebraska, Illinois, Oregon, Nevada, Maine, Virginia, Tennessee, Louisiana and most recently Massachusetts.[xxviii] The Act has been introduced in a number of states, but has yet to pass a state vote to become a law in those states.[xxix] The CROWN Act has been enacted on a local level in many cities and counties across the country, but the bill is not widespread.[xxx] As an advocate of the bill, I reached out to my local legislatures to see how a bill of sort could be introduced in the city where I live. Initially, I received little feedback and communication on the issue. However, I was happy to find out that the bill was passed in the county where I live in late 2021.[xxxi]

The question now is what is the hold up and why is the CROWN Act not being passed across the country or federally? A conclusion that can be drawn is that many of the states that refuse to enact such legislation are traditionally conservative states or states located in the south and southeastern parts of the country. States that want less government intrusion in everyday life decisions; states that have a long history of segregation, discrimination, racial tensions, and other incidents. In Nebraska, the governor vetoed the CROWN Act citing, ""The bill covers features based on mutable characteristics that are not attributable to one racial group. While hair type is an immutable characteristic, hairstyles can easily be changed. Additionally, the hairstyles named in the bill (locks, braids, and twists) are not exclusively worn by one race.""[xxxii] This thought process excludes the cultural differences that are a part of the Black race.

The laws that have passed in various states generally have the same style of language. Looking at the federal CROWN Act bill that was introduced but not passed, the language mimics the language of the state bills, giving a wider overview of the types of discriminations and the protections afforded under the CROWN Act. The CROWN Act specifically "prohibit[s] discrimination based on an individual's texture or style of hair."[xxxiii] The CROWN

Act makes the link between a person's hair needing the same type of protections that a person's race or national origin gets in prohibiting hair discrimination.[xxxiv] Protective Styles, which is the common name used in the Black community to describe braids, locs, twists, etc., is also discussed in the CROWN Act as a way of describing the hairstyles that should be protected.[xxxv]

The CROWN Act brings to the forefront the problem with the narrow interpretation of race and national origin. As mentioned in My Hair Is Professional TOO!, the judge in the pinnacle hair case, EEOC v. Catastrophe Management, discussed race to be defined as what is passed down from a parent to a child.[xxxvi] The book also discussed how the definition of race is outdated and needs to be expanded to include culture differences.[xxxvii] Cultural differences are a part of each person's race and should be included in definitions that describe race. We are not just the color of our skin or what is passed down from our parents. Our rich culture and backgrounds are as much a part of our being as the genes that make up our genetic codes. The CROWN Act also showcases how the narrow interpretation of race is the primary reason why there is a lack of protection for cultural differences such as hairstyles akin to African and Black culture.

The CROWN Act calls for the federal government to "acknowledge that individuals who have hair texture[s] or wear a hairstyle that is historically and contemporarily associated with African Americans or persons of African descent systematically suffer harmful discrimination in schools, workplaces, and other contexts based upon longstanding race and national origin stereotypes and biases."[xxxviii] The CROWN Act also calls for there to be redress based on "clear, consistent, and enforceable legal standards."[xxxix] Because the federal government plays a major role in ensuring that civil rights are enforced, the act calls on federal legislators to take up the CROWN Act to prevent widespread discrimination based on race and national origin when it comes to Black hair textures and hairstyles.[xl]

The CROWN Act's purpose, aside from protecting Black hair, is to "institute definitions of race and national origin for Federal civil rights laws that effectuate the comprehensive scope of protection Congress intended to be afforded by such laws and Congress' objective to eliminate race and national origin discrimination in the United States."[xli] The CROWN Act specifically eliminates this type of discrimination based on its purpose in federally assisted programs, housing programs, public accommodations, and in employment.[xlii] The CROWN Act gives equal protection under the laws of the United States to prohibit discrimination based on "hair texture or hairstyle if that hair texture or that hairstyle is commonly associated with a particular race or national origin (including a hairstyle in which hair is tightly coiled or tightly curled, locs, cornrows, twists, braids, Bantu knots, and Afros)."[xliii]

If passed, the CROWN Act could have sweeping consequences for employers, schools and beyond to implement policies that do not discriminate against hairstyles that are commonly associated with Black culture. States that refuse to pass these protections would have no choice but to welcome this new law and hold its employers, schools, and citizens accountable for discriminatory hair laws, policies, and practices. Many Black Americans that face discrimination daily will finally have protection under the law. These protections appear minimal but are so greatly needed. Hair discrimination is real and needs to be addressed.

The CROWN Act stands to eradicate this type of discrimination by opening a path to more equality for Black people. Typically, states that want less government intervention give more personal rights to individuals and businesses. It appears that these laws allow people to operate as they want. In states with less government, it is believed that as a business owner, an individual has or should have specific rights when it comes to their business. In our schools and places of public accommodations, less government intervention means that they are functioning as the people want or intend. This logic is flawed and does not account for the long history of discrimination and racism in America. Laws that are left vague and open for interpretation leaves too much room for intentional bias, discrimination, and racist practices.

    America needs the CROWN Act or an act like it to combat the problems that many Black Americans face. This act will give coverage and can open the door for other types of culture-based protections. It is time for America to change its laws to reflect the changes in our population. Our country needs to stop catering to one race, one group, one culture as the norm. Our norm includes many more people who deserve equal protection under the laws of this country. Right now, Black people who live in states that have not passed the Crown Act wait for legislation to be passed in their state or for the CROWN Act to be taken up by Congress. Until hair discrimination is eradicated, Black people will continue to deal with hair discrimination and the choices that must be made to conform to the societal standards of what a Black person's hair is supposed to look like.

What's In Those Products That Black People Use In Their Hair?

Black people have been forced to wear European centered hairstyles to conform to societal standards. This practice has been passed down from our parents, and oftentimes to the detriment of our health. There is growing information on the links between maintaining societal appropriate hairstyles and health concerns that harm Black people. But there has yet to be broad sweeping compensation for the people who have conformed to societal expectations and have experienced the harms related to wearing European or White hairstyles. This needs to change and more information needs to be given to the public and to the Black communities about the dangers of the products that are being used to maintain these hairstyles and on Black hair in general.

Many Black women were and, in some cases, still are accustomed to their hair being either straight or having a slick 'put together look'. Black women have used relaxers, texturizers and other chemically based products to achieve these looks. In recent years with the clean environment movement, there have been calls for more transparency in the ingredients in food and beauty products. Hair products that are targeted to and used by

Black people have taken center stage in the Black community. It is being revealed that these products may be the cause of many health problems that Black people are at a higher risk of developing.

My mother could not do hair; that was not one of her gifts. She made it known that she did not do hair. She would pay anyone to make my hair and my sister's hair look "presentable" when out in the public eye. Many women and little girls, including myself, have been getting relaxers since we were little girls. My mother relaxed my hair at a very young age. I received my first relaxer when I was under the age of 6 and I probably received a full relaxer at least twice a year and a touch up maybe once or twice in between the full relaxers. Now I feel like that probably was not the best decision. My hair has always gone through the same cycle never really growing until I completely rid myself of chemically processing of my hair.

In My Hair Is Professional TOO!, the book discussed how regular relaxers that contain lye and other chemicals can have an impact on the health of Black women. There has been an ongoing discussion and research on the use of these chemicals and their relation to uterine fibroids and other cancers. A 2017 study conducted by Rutgers University linked breast cancer to the use of relaxers.[xliv] In a study conducted by the National Institutes of Health, over 40,000 women of all races between the age of 35-74 were studied.[xlv] The study found links between relaxers, perms, and breast cancer.[xlvi] It also found that Black women are at a 45% increased risk of getting breast cancer.[xlvii]

A 2012 study in the American Journal of Epidemiology also associated the risk of fibroids with relaxers.[xlviii] Uterine fibroids "are firm, roundish, noncancerous growths in the uterus that can range in size from a pebble to a football or larger"[xlix] Black women develop them sooner than white women and the fibroids tend to be larger for Black women.[l] "In [the American Journal's recent] study of 23,000 menstruating Black American women, these participants displayed two to three times higher uterine fibroid incidences.[li] "Some estimates show that a quarter of black women between 18 and 30 have fibroids, compared with 7 percent of white women; by age 35, that number increases to 60 percent."[lii] Researchers suggest that these increases may be attributed to exposure to the chemicals in Black hair relaxers.[liii] Fibroids can have great health risks to women that have them because they can lead to "mild to severe pelvic pain, heavy periods, painful sex or urinary or bowel problems."[liv] Some women just leave them alone, but in some cases, they can lead to a woman having a hysterectomy.[lv] Because Black women are more likely to have fibroids, they are at a greater risk of having a hysterectomy during prime reproductive years.[lvi]

"According to the Silent Spring Institute, many of the hair products marketed to [B]lack women are full of harmful chemicals."[lvii] This study was conducted in 2018 and found that "the concentration of chemicals found in 18 hair products interfered with hormones."[lviii] The study also found that "84% of the toxic chemicals were not listed on the product labels."[lix] The hair relaxers label for children contained regulated or restricted chemicals.[lx]

A 2019 study also found that the use of permanent dyes increased a Black woman's risk of breast cancer by 45% compared to 7% in white women.[lxi] In a study conducted by the Environmental Working Group, which has a database of harmful products, one in twelve beauty products marketed to Black women have chemicals in them that are hazardous to the health of Black women.[lxii] The study also found that more than 25% of products that are marketed to Black women contain hazardous chemicals.[lxiii] The findings in these studies are major because it shows the casual link between the chemicals in the relaxers, Black hair products, and their prevailing use by Black women. It can be concluded that regular use of relaxers and other Black hair products cause cancer and other health risks in Black women.

This leads to the question of why these products are even on the market. There has been a long history of secret ingredients being placed in our products and foods that fall under the radar of the Food and Drug Administration (FDA).[lxiv] The FDA in some cases, especially with ingredients in foods (and the beauty industries), operates on an honor system when it comes to Generally Recognized As Safe (GRAS) ingredients.[lxv] Companies can label ingredients as GRAS and float under the radar knowing that the chemicals are harmful or that products are not being labeled correctly.[lxvi] Companies will list "acceptable" ingredients on the label but have other chemical compounds in the products.[lxvii] This is the case for hair care products too but in the hair care industry the hazardous chemicals are right in your face.[lxviii] There is little to no oversight over hair care products.[lxix] With the exception of color additives, the FDA does not approve cosmetics before they hit the shelves.[lxx] But the larger question is why products with certain chemicals are marketed to a particular group, when they should not be marketed to anyone.

In 2022, another study revealed that hair relaxers commonly used by Black women can fuel breast cancer in Black women.[lxxi] The study conducted by the City of Hope, an independent biomedical, treatment and education center, found that endocrine disrupting chemicals called parabens increase the risk of breast cancer in Black women.[lxxii] "Parabens are endocrine-disrupting chemicals that are commonly used as preservatives in hair and other personal care products. Parabens cause breast cancer cells to grow, invade, spread and express genes linked to cancer and to hormone action."[lxxiii] The study revealed that Black women are at a greater risk of developing cancer under the age of 40.[lxxiv] American women usually do not get their first mammogram until age 40.[lxxv] That puts Black women behind the ball of even finding out if they have Breast Cancer, which can mean Black women may find out when it's too late. Black women and Black people in general are often not included in testing samples.[lxxvi] Black people tend to find out later or not at all about things that are a detriment to their health and wellbeing.[lxxvii]

In another study released in late 2022, the National Institute of Environmental Health Sciences (NIH) found that chemical hair-straightening products put women at a higher risk of uterine cancer.[lxxviii] The studied reviewed the hair care routines of 33,000 women who used these products at least 4 times a year and found that those women were two times more likely to develop uterine cancer.[lxxix] As with the City of Hope study, "chemicals like parabens, phthalates and fragrances in hair care products disrupt the endocrine system, which helps regulate hormones.[lxxx] This leads to the growth of cancers.[lxxxi] The study also identified that 60 percent of the participants were Black women.[lxxxii] Companies are making millions of dollars every year and Black women are suffering. As more and more Black owned products make their way to shelves, using the same types of chemicals, we must be concerned that Black business owners in the hair industry are also contributing to the demise of the health of Black people if they are following the status quo.

To bring a legal claim for damages, you must first have an injury. You then must identify the cause of the injury. Once you find the cause, you must make a link between the injury and the person or entity that caused the injury. In the case of relaxers, we must show that a person used relaxers, then developed breast cancer and that the relaxer was the cause of the breast cancer. Studies like those mentioned, can provide evidence and support to show the link between the chemicals in the products and the development of cancers. It is unfortunate that in some cases, particularly class action lawsuits, this evidence and the harm can be buried in a lawsuit if the lawsuit settles before going to trial. In other cases, a company will put parameters or limitations on your ability to sue them by "bar[ing] consumers from suing them in federal court, and instead forc[ing] victims to pursue arbitration or, in some cases, fil[ing] suit[s] in small claims court." [lxxxiii]

There are cases where the public finds out that a company has caused a great harm, and some people get monetary settlements, but the company usually does not formally admit to the harm. They just pay the bill and continue to knowingly produce products that cause these harms. Companies will do a cost analysis before knowingly putting a harmful product on the market. If the company will make more money than the amount that they would have to pay out for injuries, some companies may choose to move forward with products despite knowing the harm the product may cause.[lxxxiv] They just hope to not get caught. Companies have also used the bankruptcy court as a means of escaping liability or delaying paying money that they should be required to pay.[lxxxv] However, with the recent findings linking the chemicals in hair products to cancers and fibroids major lawsuits are soon to follow.

Hair companies are continuing to make money at the expense of the health of its customers, knowingly. In the 2022 Television series, Not So Pretty, it was revealed just how harmful the chemicals used in these products are. The series also shed light on the number of toxic ingredients being used in the United States compared to other countries. The European Union (EU) has banned or restricted more than 1,300 chemicals while the United States has outlawed or curbed just 11.[lxxxvi] There have been great strides to get the United States Congress to pass legislation banning harmful chemicals, but bills tend to stall out like the CROWN Act legislation.[lxxxvii] California is the only state to have legislation requiring companies to report harmful ingredients used in cosmetics.[lxxxviii]

According to Essence Magazine, the Black hair industry is an estimated $2.5 billion a year industry.[lxxxix] Money is a driving factor for companies to do many things good and bad. In the case of Black hair, capitalizing off an already vulnerable population is easy and at the same time troubling. Black women are vulnerable because they are constantly judged based on their appearance, particularly their hair. Striving to achieve a certain look can take its toll on the Black community particularly when the images you are striving for are not of your culture and in many cases are flawed. A then and now article was passed around social media showing the kids that were the face of the relaxer boxes in the 1990's.[xc] The various posts showed side by side pictures of the kids on the relaxer box and a picture of them as an adult today.[xci] It was revealed that many of the models on the relaxer boxes marketed to Black people that contain harmful chemicals had not used the relaxers in their hair for the photos on the product packaging.[xcii] The revelation took the Black community aback and many felt that they had been bamboozled by the false advertising.[xciii]

Black women using products that are hazardous to their health knowingly and unknowingly is happening because in many cases, it could be the difference between having a job to survive and provide for yourself verses not. Not only is it troubling that Black women are being capitalized on at the expense of their health, but it is also a financial burden. The financial burden disadvantages Black women because it tends to cost more to maintain Black hair. Not to mention the amount of time spent getting and maintaining appropriate styles. Black hair products tend to be more expensive and tend to have long processes to use. Black women spend hours and sometimes days to make their hair look presentable.[xciv] Black women often joke about a "wash-n-go" being just as time consuming as any other style. Overtime, Black women are spending more money and using more of their time to make their appearance presentable.[xcv] It can also be argued that they are not enjoying life to the fullest because they must be concerned about maintaining their look. A Black woman getting her hair wet could mean a trip back to the beautician to achieve the presentable look, which means more time and more money.

Black women and Black people in general who use these

products do not have a strong hold in the hair industries that supply and market these products.[xcvi] In order for a Black hair brand to scale their businesses or grow, they seek outside investors which opens the door for other non-Black companies to buyout or take over the Black owned company.[xcvii] This can lead to the diminishing of the integrity of the product ingredients. Black people are further left with little to no legal ramifications for the damage these products have caused or will cause. Until October of 2022, there had not been a major headline class action lawsuit for Black people against companies that use chemicals that are harmful to a Black person's hair.[xcviii] Black people continue to be forced to conform to beauty standards set by society that are detrimental to the health of Black women.

There are several organizations that have tried to bring awareness to the dangers of chemicals in our everyday products. Environmental Working Group (EWG) is one such company. EWG has compiled lists of products and rates them on a scale of 1-10 based on their level of toxicity.[xcix] A simple search for hair gels, which are frequently used by Black women and men to achieve a frozen natural hair look with wash and go hairstyles, identified that many of the hair gels targeted to Black men and women rated at a 4 or above on their level of toxicity.[c] This is one example that furthers the point that many of the products that Black people use to achieve a more presentable look for society can be hazardous to their health.

It's worth mentioning that the curly hair movement is different from the black woman curly girl natural hair movement. These movements are distinguishable because the curly girl movement gained traction with white women who had curly hair and wanted to make their curly hair fit into society. The Black natural hair movement is distinguishable because, Black people are trying to make their natural hair and hairstyles, like afros, braids, locs, twists, bantu knots, etc., become common place in society.[ci] It should also be noted that Black hair that is curlier or of a softer texture is more accepted in society than thicker, kinkier or more course textured afro hair. This is commonly referred to as good hair verses bad or nappy hair in the Black community. The softer curls appear less threatening but are still not fully accepted in society when worn by Black people. But the two movements are different. Both affect women who have hair that is not European straight, one is more accepted than the other. While wearing an Afro hairstyle cannot legally be discriminated against no matter the texture, that does not stop the discrimination or implicit bias. Because hairstyles akin to African culture may be best suited for many Black hair textures, it is imperative that the CROWN Act is passed.

Recently in the state of Louisiana, where the CROWN Act is now law, some hair policies have changed in the hair care industry. The Louisiana Board of Cosmetology added a section to their licensing exam to include Black hair maintenance. [cii] This is believed to be a step toward equality in the industry. This can be seen as both a step towards equality and/or another means of taking over the industry from the Black community of hairstylist. In the hair care industry, many feel that it is important for stylist to be able to style all types of hair, including Black natural hair. This has been a concern in the entertainment industry for some time.[ciii] Many Black women come to work to record movies and television shows with their hair already done or bring their own stylist because of the inability of the white hairstylist to style Black hair.[civ] Even though these white stylists have not traditionally taken on doing black hair, they would still get movie credits for wardrobe even though the hair was styled by someone else or the actress came to set with their hair already done.

Even with this information, the passage of laws that ban hair discrimination, and society gaining knowledge about the impacts of conforming to societal standards, the discrimination persists. People say well you have a choice to put a relaxer in your hair, or you have a choice to wear your hair as you choose, but it is not that simple. We are literally deciding between conforming to discriminatory standards, the right to gain an education, being able to provide for ourselves and families through gainful employment and being healthy or losing our self-identity. The beauty industry that enables Black women to maintain these hairstyles remains largely unregulated.[cv] Black women are being left at the mercy of these companies because they are having to maintain a look that could ultimately have an impact on their quality of life. One should not have to make these types of decisions when the choice involves conforming to standards that were set to be exclusive and those standards have a detrimental effect on a person's life and health. The lack of oversight and liability in the hair care industry should be alarming to us all.

Now: Recent Hair Discrimination Stories In The Workplace

There has been a great push towards getting the CROWN Act or similar legislation passed by advocates on the state and local levels. It has worked in some places, but we are far from done in many others. Because there is no protection in many areas of the country, discrimination based on how a person styles their hair is still happening. The first national headline case to seek protection under the CROWN Act occurred in a state where the CROWN Act is law. Depending on which state you live in, there is little recourse for many people facing this type of discrimination.

In California a movie company is seeing the first major claim of protection under the CROWN Act.[cvi] A San Diego Black male Jeffrey Thornton, claimed that he was denied employment after he refused to trim his locs. Thornton was employed with Encore Group for four years prior to being furloughed due to the COVID-19 Pandemic in Florida.[cvii] He moved to San Diego with the intention of returning to his position once the work operations resumed.[cviii] In October of 2021, he received an email requesting that he reach out to Encore to return to work.[cix] Over the course of Thornton's time in furlough, his locs had grown substantially.[cx] Thornton requested and attended an interview for the position of Technical Supervisor.[cxi] He was told that he was fully qualified for the position, but he would have to conform to the dress and appearance policies which restricted jewelry, tattoos and the appearance of facial hair, Thornton agreed.[cxii] However, Encore requested that Thornton cut his hair so that it was off his ears, eyes and shoulders, stating that using a hair-tie would not be enough.[cxiii]

The Encore company policy was vague. It stated that hair had to be "clean, neat and styled." Thornton claimed that for him to conform to the policy, he "would have to materially alter his hairstyle, and thus his appearance, cultural identity, and racial heritage."[cxiv] His failure to comply ended in an all too familiar ending; he was denied the position. In the lawsuit, Thornton seeks damages for discrimination based on race and failure to prevent discrimination under the CROWN Act.[cxv] The response from the company called the incident a "misunderstanding" of what the manager said and stated that Thornton was welcomed to rejoin the company.[cxvi] The company also stated that they are ""reviewing [their] grooming policies to avoid potential miscommunications in the future.""[cxvii]

The vague language in grooming policies operate as a way of discriminating against employees under the guise of neutral grooming policies.[cxviii] One such policy that uses vague language is the 2021 grooming policy by United Airlines. These policies are not unusual for the airline industry.[cxix] In the 1980's, American Airlines won a pinnacle case in the hair discrimination battle when a court ruled that the airline company could maintain a hair policy that prohibited braids.[cxx] United Airlines' new hair policy allows for hair length to go past the shoulder, however, the policy still uses vague language.[cxxi] The policy states that the "hair must be at shoulder length or shorter, and must still be kept "neat and tidy.""[cxxii] The words "neat and tidy" leaves room for interpretation and discrimination. When examining such policies, we must ask whose perception of "neat and tidy" will be used and what hairstyles will be deemed "neat and tidy."

In New Orleans, a lawsuit was filed against Shreveport-based American Screening LLC, for firing a woman for wearing her natural hair.[cxxiii] In 2018, a black woman was hired while wearing a wig styled in a White or European look.[cxxiv] She later stopped wearing the wig and began to wear her natural hair, usually in a bun.[cxxv] "The lawsuit alleges that the owner complained to managers, including the human resources manager, that the employee "came in with beautiful hair" but now "looks like she rolls out of bed.""[cxxvi] The premise of the lawsuit is that other women wear ponytails and buns to work just as the Black woman did. The employer did not complain about the other women wearing the same hairstyle but did complain about the Black woman because of her natural hair texture. This is a case of outright hair discrimination; the CROWN Act was not the law in the state of Louisiana or New Orleans at the time. However, a new city ordinance enacted in December of 2020 and the recent enactment of the CROWN Act in the state makes this type of hair discrimination illegal.[cxxvii]

In Columbus, Ohio, prominent Black women in a video shared instances of hair discrimination.[cxxviii] Ohio Representative Juanita Brent shared how concerned her campaign staff was when she decided to wear braids in her political ads.[cxxix] She was told by many that straight hair was expected of her in her role.[cxxx] She shared how people felt that braids are not what is expected from a Black woman politician.[cxxxi] The CROWN Act is now a city ordinance in Columbus.[cxxxii] In Dallas, Texas, Judge Amber Givens spoke of her natural hair being politicized.[cxxxiii] She was told that she would offend voters by wearing her natural hair in her pursuit to be the next Dallas County judge.[cxxxiv]

A Dallas police officer, Dakari Davis, spoke on how his braided hair was deemed unprofessional by one of his superior officers.[cxxxv] A formal complaint was filed against his cornrows hairstyle as well as an internal investigation.[cxxxvi] The refusal of Davis to cut his hair led to him being "placed on paid administrative leave, a recommendation for termination, and a letter of reprimand."[cxxxvii] Davis ended up cutting his hair because he was fearful of being retaliated against.[cxxxviii] After an intervention with the Dallas County Commissioner, several months later the letter of reprimand was rescinded.[cxxxix] No one should be fired for wearing braids, specifically when the hairstyle has no bearing on the person's ability to perform the tasks of the job. People like Davis are being fired based on a personal preference rooted in racial bias.[cxl] When Davis responds to a call to save a person's life, that person is not going to question his braided hairstyle.

In Sonoma, California, Bianca Ruffin went on a job interview at MacArthur Place Inn & Spa.[cxli] According to Ruffin the human resources manager at the hotel stated that her natural hair was inappropriate for the position where she would be customer facing.[cxlii] Ruffin who had natural []locs was shocked by the comments and posted her experience on the yelp and Facebook under the company's name.[cxliii] The vice president of human resources for the hotel, responded citing an "unfortunate miscommunication" about the company's policy.[cxliv] Ruffin spoke with another human resources representative and was told that locs were not prohibited and that the company welcomed them.[cxlv] Ruffin was later contacted and offered the job but she declined.[cxlvi] In California the CROWN Act is law. It makes sense that the company attempted to make this situation right. Ruffin stated that she was considering filing a complaint because of the occurrence.[cxlvii]

The United States Army recently changed its grooming policy to allow ponytails in all uniforms. The Army has been slow to amend its hair policies but changed its stance on some forms of locs in 2017.[cxlviii] The change opened the door for soldiers to wear "a bun, single ponytail, two braids or a single braid; loc[]s, braids, twists or cornrows can come together in one or two braids or a ponytail; and braids or a ponytail can go as far down as the bottom of the shoulder blades."[cxlix]The policy change came after 12 year veteran Jessica Sims was discharge from her post after refusing to cut her locs.[cl] Sims wore her locs in a bun hairstyle.[cli] She was told that her hair prohibited her from using certain equipment such as gas masks and safety helmets.[clii] Sims demonstrated that she could use the equipment without occurrence, but it was not good enough to allow her to keep her post.[cliii] These are just a few of the publicized cases of hair discrimination in America that has led to loss of employment. This should not happen, particularly when you are able to perform your job with your hairstyle.[cliv]

Hair discrimination continues to be a problem in America and globally. However, many Black people are owning their natural hair textures and styles that are akin to African culture. Black women are taking their experiences of hair discrimination and using it as fuel to continue their natural hair journeys, in the workplace and in life.[clv] Many women are embracing their natural hair and finding creative ways to fit their hair and hairstyles into society. Karine Jean-Pierre made history as the first openly gay and only the second Black woman to lead a White House press briefing.[clvi] At the briefing she wore her hair in a short afro with blond highlights in the front.[clvii] She was later named White House Press Secretary, wearing the same natural hair style.[clviii] The new Justice to the United States Supreme Court, Justice Ketanji Brown Jackson, who wears her hair in locs, was confirmed to the highest court. When Justice Brown was grilled by members of Congress on her impeccable legal career, no one asked if her hair would prohibit her from doing her job. Justice Brown showed the world that Black natural hair is definitely Professional TOO!

At the unveiling of the Obama's official portraits at the White House, Michelle Obama wore braids tucked into a bun.[clix] It was a powerful and bold move towards showing the world that hairstyles akin to African culture can fit into any setting.

The braided style did not go unnoticed, as social media lit up in response to the former first lady's choice of hairstyle.[clx] This global moment again put the spotlight on hair discrimination and the lack of legal protections the average person has when wearing hairstyles akin to African culture. Hair discrimination leaves little recourse for those who face it and do not have protections under the law.

    The idea that it is just hair, and that Black people should just conform to get, keep, and advance on the job is not holding weight anymore. There is a battle between those that are okay with conforming and those who want to embrace their natural hair and hairstyles akin to African culture. For an employer, if you have a group willing to conform no matter the expense or detriment to their health, the employer is more attuned to agreeing with the position of conformity. This makes the plight to equality harder for those that choose to wear their natural hair textures and hairstyles akin to African culture. We cannot be okay with any type of hair discrimination no matter who it is perpetuated against.

MY HAIR IS STILL PROFESSIONAL TOO! WHERE ARE WE NOW?

APRIL MARIA WILLIAMS

Respectability Politics: Making The Natural Hair Plight Harder?

Respectability politics are good and bad depending on your views in society and what your beliefs are as to how you should fit into society. Far too often the Black community finds their way at the center of respectability politics because we are always being judged for how we do or do not fit into what society deems as appropriate. A Black person's hair is no different. There is always discussion within the Black community and outside of it as to what a Black person's hair is supposed to look like to be considered presentable.

Never could I have imagined that I would be contemplating how I was going to wear my hair for my law school graduation photos. It wasn't even something I thought to be a major deal. In our third year of law school, we have our school photos. One photo is of the student in their cap and gown and the other is your professional photo. Your cap and gown photo would be the photo that will be on display in the school for now and until the end of eternity. Your professional photo would ideally be used as your first professional photo as a JD or an Esquire. The month before the photos were to take place, the conversation among all the natural hair students began to start. Are you going to wear your hair relaxed straight, in braids or in an afro? Relaxed straight hair, the more acceptable hair standard in the American workplace, was of course the hair style of choice. More so because of societal pressures of what looks presentable as opposed to what we looked like on a regular basis.

I chose to wear my hair in a less dramatic afro hair style. When I made the decision to wear my afro, I distinctly remember one of my classmates being mortified at the thought of me wearing my afro in my professional photos. To be clear, there is nothing wrong with women wearing their hair straight if they choose to, it's the thought that a Black woman must make the decision based on what is acceptable to someone else in the workplace and in society. No one should have to choose between straight hair and their natural textures and styles to be accepted in society. I decided that people were either going to love it or not. My resume would speak for itself and if that was not good enough, then maybe that job or position was not for me. I want to work and be around people who accept me for me, including my natural kinky hair.

Sometimes it's the pressure from members of the Black community that project bias societal standards on other Black people. In the summer of 2021, the popular actress and comedian Monique made a viral post speaking on Black women having pride in their appearance by not wearing bonnets and pajamas in the airport. Her comments struck a nerve in the Black community and re-sparked ongoing conversations on what has been coined as respectability politics. Respectability politics is the argument that not conforming to what society deems acceptable is considered disrespectful.[clxi] It's the idea that one will deny or not care to consider their own cultural differences to conform to what society at large expects, even when conforming or accepting societal standards can be discriminatory against the conformer. It's allowing one group to deem something acceptable for all and condemning those that chose not to fit into the standards. The standard that is set is molded by and made for the majority not really to be inclusive of the marginalized group or groups the standards can discriminate against.

The idea of what hair styles are acceptable is often dictated by what Black women and Black men are willing to accept as professional and appropriate. Black people maintain these standards to reach Black excellence as a minority in society. But even when conforming, it does not at times stop the outright discrimination faced each day.[clxii] If Black people collectively say, we accept styles akin to African culture and straight hair styles, it is less likely that our hairstyles will not be accepted in society. As long as Black people are willing to fit in, and accept discrimination based on hair style, there is no need for society as a whole to change their views or to be more inclusive. By conforming, accepting, and promoting the standards that are discriminatory, the conformer, acceptor and promotor becomes a part of the overall problem.

In my view, what is respectable in the Black community is a standard that has been created by Black people, at times based in white ideals of who and what Black people should be to be accepted. Typically, Black people are the arbiters of what is respectable in the Black community. But it is based on how we want to be perceived in our society, not from the eyes of Black culture, but from the eyes of White culture. Black people want to be accepted by all communities and all members of society. To be accepted that means at times you must be willing to sacrifice your own cultural identity to fit in. That mindset disadvantages Black people and opens the door for those who do not want to sacrifice their cultural identities to be discriminated against or penalized by society at large. Even for naturally occurring parts of our identities such as one's hair texture.

A prime example of this is pants sagging. The origins of pants sagging come from the prison system where men were not given belts or strings to hold up their pants which resulted in sagging. It is also believed that men in prison who purposely sagged their pants where open to sexual relations with the same sex. In the 90's, pants sagging was associated with gang culture and the idea that one was uncaring as to their appearance. In recent years, pop culture has embraced pants sagging as a fashion trend. It is now a style and a choice based on a person's fashion sense. However, it has been generally acknowledged by the Black community that pants sagging is not acceptable, meaning sagging your pants is not acceptable to fit into societal standards. Because of this lack of acceptability, it has been criminalized in cities across the country. In Opalocka, FL and Shreveport City, LA there were laws that made sagging illegal and had penalties that could resulted in a person going to jail.[clxiii] In Opalocka, FL and Shreveport City, LA the laws were deemed illegal because it was found to disproportionally affect Black people, Black men in particular. But the idea that what is deemed "respectable" does not cause any real harm is a fallacy because it has resulted in Black people being put in jail.[clxiv] Can you imagine a person being jailed for their hairstyle? When Black people set certain standards many times, we don't understand how detrimental it can be to Black people trying find space in society that is accepting of who we are.

Black people set standards in our communities that put us in a position of judgment based on a standard that was not created for or by Black people. Those standards are in turn weaponized against Black people and in many cases affects our ability to navigate without discrimination and can at times be used to criminalize Black people. Many times, this is not seen or understood because, these standards have long since been accepted as a norm of a society that has historically discriminated or excluded Black people. Norms that have negatively impacted and affected the Black Community.

However, as with pants sagging, when other groups can monetize off something that once was deemed inappropriate, it becomes more accepting by society. Even when society accepts what was once deemed inappropriate, Black people will still uphold the standard oftentimes to our detriment. Kim Kardashian wore Fulani braids to an award show and made front page for her "fashioned" hair.[clxv] She even renamed the traditional African hairstyle.[clxvi] This was a classic case of monetization off a Black culture when Black women and children across the globe have been and continue to be discriminated against for wearing the very same style.[clxvii] It burns deep when Black people can face backlash for something over and over, only for it to be accepted when culturally appropriated or used to make money for others.

We have grown accustomed to accepting standards not made by us to be appeasing to people who fail to or choose not to understand the negative impacts of such standards. These standards oftentimes shame or ignore the little history that Black people know about themselves. Hair discrimination continues to show its face in our everyday lives and most recently in our schooling systems against Black children.

APRIL MARIA WILLIAMS

Now: Hair Discrimination Stories In Schools

Hair discrimination is not exclusive to the workplace. In recent years, there has been public outcry to school boards and administrations for their discriminatory school handbooks and policies. Some policies are outright discriminatory, and others use vague language left open for discriminatory interpretation. This problem is having a negative impact on Black kids at these schools. Kids are being disciplined, suspended, and not allowed to participate in school events because of their hairstyle. Kids are being told to cut their locs and braids because it does not conform to dress code policies. The CROWN Act or similar legislation is needed to protect the future of our kids from these damaging consequences in schools.

When I was a kid, I hated getting my hair done. Again, my mom, by all accounts was no beautician. I hated when my mom did my hair, because I never knew what the result would be or if I would have to show up to school with a big burn mark on my forehead from the curling iron. My hair was relaxed like some of my friends. She would also pay people to do my hair, but I played hard, and my hair never stayed in its place. My hair not staying in place, I attribute to my mom trying to maintain straight hairstyles with ponytails and straight hair twists in my hair.

Over the summers she would pay people to braid my hair. I preferred braids because it meant that I would not have to sit every other day to get my hair done. When I had my braids, I could go almost the whole summer without having to take away from my playtime and summer freedom. The braids also made it easier for me to go swimming without my hair being out of place the next day, even after washing my hair with the braids. I realize now that my hair often grew longer while in braids because I was not constantly tugging and pulling at it. I was also not subjected to relaxers during the periods that I wore braids.

But then the school year would come around and my mom would take me to the beautician to relax my hair, get it done up, only for it to last for a few days before she would resort back to putting the braids in for a short period. The cycle was the same during the school year, straight hair, then braids, then back to straight hair. Some of my school pictures did not always look the best. Despite my hair woes, I never got in trouble for wearing my various hairstyles in school, even when some of the styles could have been considered "extreme". We sometimes wore braids, big ponytails in the "fan" style (it literally looked like a half fan, google it), and wearing colored hair was never looked at as out of the ordinary. There was a time that my sister tried to dye her hair Blonde, but it turned orange and the only person that had a problem with it was my mom. We lived in an inner-city urban neighborhood in New Jersey which was more liberal and diverse.

School policies have become a big deal in recent years. Today a Black child's hairstyle has made national news headlines with administrators, school officials and school athletic officials taking dramatic measures to penalize or exclude kids for their style. Kids are being sent home, suspended, and put into in-school suspension for not conforming to school policies that are race and gender insensitive or just outright discriminatory. For as long as

I can remember, at no time has a child's hairstyle garnered this much controversy.

The CROWN Act's research in connection with the brand Dove, found that "53% of Black mothers say their daughters have experienced race-based hair discrimination as early as five years old."[clxviii] By age 10, a Black girl that attends a majority-white school will experience hair discrimination.[clxix] At some point 66% of Black children that attend majority-white school will experience hair discrimination.[clxx] This form of discrimination comes from school policies and microaggressions from teachers and students. Hair discrimination has a major impact on the student's well-being and experience while in school settings and school related functions.[clxxi]

There are some who feel that these policies are needed and that schools have a right to implement dress code policies for students. In New Orleans at Christ the King Parish School, a school policy specifically addresses hair extensions stating, "[h]air (including cuts, colors, and styles) should not interfere with the learning process or values being upheld at Christ the King School . . . Hairstyles for boys and girls should be neat, clean, conservative, and the natural color at all times."[clxxii] The handbook further states that "uniform dress produces good behavior and morale . . . [and] gives each student equal standing among his or her peers, regardless of economic background.[clxxiii] While Christ the King Parish is a catholic school and may not necessarily fall into the same purview as public schools, they are not allowed to discriminate based on race.[clxxiv] However, other schools have followed suit under the premise that, one should expect stricter policies when attending a catholic school.[clxxv] The handbook specifically bans students from wearing extensions, wigs and hairpieces, only natural hair is allowed.[clxxvi]

It is believed that because the policy tells you to come to school with your hair as you were born, it automatically translates to the policy not being discriminatory. But that logic, is just as tone deaf, as the policy itself. It lacks the understanding of what Black people go through when trying to make themselves look presentable in a society dominated by white beauty and professional standards. It ignores how sometimes just wearing an afro can also damage a Black persons' hair. The policy ignores, what it truly means for a Black people to wear their hair completely natural (no relaxer).[clxxvii] Protective styles are sometimes needed to protect natural hair from damage, which is again ignored by these policies.[clxxviii] Anytime a law or policy has a disproportionate effect on one class of people and that policy is not for safety or health reasons, that policy should be examined to really see why and how that group is affected. An examination would be a conversation starter and a start to creating inclusion for those who are impacted. Because of the impact on Black people, these policies can no longer be accepted as societal norms.

In 2019, New Jersey saw these hair policies play out at a school wrestling match. Andrew Johnson was targeted by a high school wrestling official for wearing his hair in locs at a wrestling match.[clxxix] A viral video captured a wrestling referee official cutting Johnson's locs out of his head prior to competing in his match.[clxxx] Johnson was told to cut his locs in order to compete because they did not conform to their policies or forfeit the competition.[clxxxi] The official that made the call had previously been accused of calling another official a racial slur, but was supported by followers who cited that he was just "enforcing the rules."[clxxxii] Even after a state civil rights investigation was opened, Johnson and his attorney still cited that he was facing backlash from the fallout of the whole ordeal.[clxxxiii] Johnson who had taken a break from competing because the incident made national headlines, came back to more controversy over his hair again in order to compete.[clxxxiv] This time Johnson was told that he had to cover his hair in order to compete.[clxxxv] When the official was question as to why he had to cover his hair, Johnson was told that they mistook him for another player and was allowed to compete.[clxxxvi]

This was not the only incident in 2019 that called a student's choice of hairstyle in question. In Texas, a six-year-old elementary school student, Johnathan Brown, was sent home from school for violating the school's dress code policy.[clxxxvii] He wore his hair in locs and was told that his hair needed to be cut.[clxxxviii] His mother took to social media to vent her frustrations with the school's policy and treatment of her son.[clxxxix] Throughout the school year her son had not received a complaint about his hair and her son stated that he loved his hair.[cxc] The notice about Brown's hair came right before Christmas break.[cxci] The notice stated that the school expected compliance upon Brown's return from break.[cxcii] His mother felt that the policy was discriminatory based on race and sex.[cxciii] She sent her son back to school with his hair unchanged after the Christmas break.[cxciv] Brown was sent to the school's office and school officials discussed Brown's hair with him.[cxcv] Apparently, they talked with the six year old about his hair and being on the news (without his mother being present).[cxcvi] In that conversation Brown went from loving his hair to wanting to cut it and asked his mother to not say mean things about people on television.[cxcvii] The administrators responded by saying that they sent similar flyers home to parents about their student's hair, citing that hair length was the issue, not the locs.[cxcviii]

The policy at Brown's school stated that a boy's hair may not be lower than the bottom of the ears or collar and may not touch the eyebrows.[cxcix] The policy further banned boys from having ponytails, buns and pinned up styles.[cc] This statement alone is problematic as we know that girls are allowed to have ponytails, buns and pinned up styles.[cci] There can be no sex discrimination even when the offensive party is just a child.[ccii] The policy stated that hairstyles that are distracting where not allowed.[cciii] The question is what hairstyles are considered distracting? Subjective inserts into any policy or law opens the door for discrimination because the policy or law is left to the interpretation of the person in the position of authority. Brown's parents started a petition on Change.org to stop the school from committing this type of discrimination.[cciv]

In another Texas story that made national headlines, De'Andre Arnold was disciplined at school for wearing his hair in locs. In Barbers Hill School District, which is only 3% Black, the school policy did not allow longer hair for male students.[ccv] Arnold had previously followed the school dress code, until the school board decided to make the code stricter, making the students adhere to hair length requirements.[ccvi] The new standards would require Arnold to cut his hair. Arnold was told that he would not be able to attend school prom or walk in his graduation ceremony if he did not adhere to the policy.[ccvii] His mother, who felt the policy was discriminatory, withdrew her son from the school and transferred him to another school district.[ccviii] Arnold's cousin, Kaden Bradford, who also wears locs was targeted by the school because of his hairstyle.[ccix] He was told by the same school that he would be suspended if he did not cut his hair.[ccx] Bradford's family decided to fight back and won the right for Bradford to wear his locs.[ccxi] In court it was argued by Professor D. Wendy Greene, a pioneer in eradicating hair discrimination and the drafting of the CROWN Act, that Bradford's hair was a part of his race, culture and heritage.[ccxii] Greene used historical and sociological evidence to support her argument.[ccxiii] A federal court ruled that the policy was discriminatory.[ccxiv]

Also in Texas, an elementary student Maddox Cozart, was constantly pulled out of class and given in-school suspension for wearing hairstyles that are representative of his culture.[ccxv] Cozart is Black, White, and Native American. He wore his hair with the top in cornrow braids and the side edged into a fade style.[ccxvi] The school stated that the style did not conform to the policy which prohibited boys from wearing ponytails, top knots, buns, or similar styles.[ccxvii] Again, this policy not only discriminates based on race and culture, but it also discriminates based on gender.[ccxviii]

In 2022, a Texas teen Dyree Williams who has worn braids and twist all his life, found himself on the receiving end of a discriminatory school policy when he moved from Ohio to Texas.[ccxix] The East Bernard Independent School District policy prohibits braided hair or cornrows.[ccxx] The school's handbook also states, "[b]oy's hair may not extend below the eyebrows, below the tops of the ears or below a conventional standup shirt collar, and must not be more than one-inch difference in the length of the hair on the side to the length of the hair on top."[ccxxi] "The handbook goes on to state that,

> "This includes but [is] not limited to tall hair styles, side swept bang styles, and long hair dangling over shaved sides or shaved back of the head. This also includes mullets and mullets in the making. Braided hair or corn rows will not be allowed. No extreme in hair styles."[ccxxii]

Williams' mother met with school administrators in person to discuss the matter to no avail.[ccxxiii] A religious exemption was filed on behalf of Williams, but it was denied.[ccxxiv] In this case, there are multiple concerns, including the outright sex discrimination based on hair length, hair discrimination based on hair styles akin to African culture and discrimination based on religious beliefs. One would think that these policies would be struck down before they are implemented but they are unfortunately commonplace in school policies.

Williams' case is like the De'Andre Arnold case, except for the addition of the denial for religious reasons. This is troubling because it appears that the school is making its own determination of a person's religious beliefs when it comes to hair. A person's hair can have religious and spiritual meaning, which should not be discounted or ignored. Williams' mother asked the school for clarification on the denial but has yet to hear back from the school.[ccxxv] After this story made news headlines, the school removed the handbook from their website.[ccxxvi]

Dyree Williams is far from alone in being punished for hair in Texas schools as of late. In May of 2022, Treyvion Gray was suspended from a Needville Independent School District located in Fort Bend County Texas because of the length of his locs.[ccxxvii] He was also told he could not walk at his graduation.[ccxxviii] Gray was told to cut his hair to conform to the hair policy that requires boys' hair to "not cover their ears, past their eyebrows, "or over the top of a standard collar in the back when combed down.""[ccxxix] Gray feels that his locs are a part of his cultural identity and that racial discrimination is at play in his punishment.[ccxxx] Because the school is discriminating based on length of hair, discrimination based on sex is also a concern in this case.

Some of these instances has led to lawsuits being filed and fueled the introduction of the CROWN Act by the Texas Legislatures in 2020. However, the importance of the CROWN Act has yet to be acknowledged as Texas legislatures have failed to pass the bill. The American Civil Liberties Union sent letters to the 500 school districts in Texas asking them to change their unconstitutional and discriminatory policies.[ccxxxi] The letter specifically states that the policies related to the hair lengths for males were harmful and outdated.[ccxxxii] As we can see with the recent case of discrimination against Dyree Williams, schools are not willing to change the policies unless forced to do so by public pressure or laws requiring them to change.

These school policies while, appearing to be race and gender neutral (based on outdated norms), they are everything but. Not only are these policies subjective to the person interpreting the policy, but they are also racially and culturally discriminatory and, in some cases, discriminatory based on gender and religion. These hair policies automatically expect Black kids to conform, forgetting or neglecting the fact that there are differences between a white person's hair texture and a Black person's hair texture. But really, we must understand that hair is hair. For Black hair to be considered normal, schools need to stop making policies that exclude and make policies that are more inclusive to all.

In 2021, the National Federation of State High Schools Association amended its discriminatory policy after North Carolina sophomore Nicole Pyles was forced to cut her hair during a softball game.[ccxxxiii] Plyes, who was wearing braids and beads[ccxxxiv], was first told that her hair was covering her jersey.[ccxxxv] She was then told that her beads were prohibited.[ccxxxvi] She told her friends to cut her hair and take the beads out right on the spot so that she could participate.[ccxxxvii] The policy did not make mention of hairstyle but did specifically ban hair beads.[ccxxxviii] Beads, in many sports, are not allowed because they pose a risk to athletes should the beads fall out. Plyes' parents who were not at the game during the incident were rightfully upset. Plyes stated she was embarrassed and upset but complied to compete.[ccxxxix] In the associations' decision to amend its rules, they understood that the restrictive rules had the effect of discriminating based on cultural backgrounds.[ccxl] The association also had a rule in its books that required prior approval for head coverings that were worn for religious reasons.[ccxli] That rule also has since been changed.[ccxlii]

In Chicago, Gus "Jett" Hawkins was disciplined at Providence St. Mel, a catholic school, for violating his school's hair policy.[ccxliii] Gus who was four years old wore his hair in braids with a ponytail and bun style.[ccxliv] The school's policy, stated that Afros or short hairstyles were allowed but hairstyles such as braids, locs or twist were not.[ccxlv] This story gained the attention of the Illinois Senator Mike Simmons who drafted the Jett Hawkins Act.[ccxlvi] The Act would prohibit this type of hair discrimination and would require a probe into schools handbooks to make sure that this type of discrimination was not present.[ccxlvii] The CROWN Act was later passed in the state of

Illinois which makes it illegal to have policies that discriminate based on hairstyles culturally associated with Black people. The Illinois State Board of Education has taken the initiative to educate school officials on "the law and hairstyles historically associated with race, ethnicity, or hair texture" to ensure compliance.[ccxlviii]

These instances have raised the question of whether schools should be allowed to tell students how they can dress and wear their hair to school. School policies are made to ensure that education is carried out in a safe and orderly manner. At what point does the school's policy reach the level of discrimination. These policies can be seen as the start to grooming kids or shaping their minds into conformity as they grow. Comply no matter what the cost or be punished. Teaching them to not question authority, even when that authority is a clear violation of their rights. If children are told as a child that their hair is not welcomed or accepted, not only does it lower their self-esteem, but it teaches them that what is important to them, their appearance, does not matter unless you look the way someone else wants you to. It strips our children of their cultural roots as well as their individualism. If your culture and individualism is taken away from you as a child, you are easily conformed. The child grows up being okay with their rights being violated, even when their health is at risk. This is especially troubling when you are being punished for exercising a constitutional right and the punishment for not conforming can have deep impacts on a child's future.

In another case of school administrators taking a child's hair into their own hands, a school secretary cut the hair of two girl's without the permission of their parents.[ccxlix] The two girls are members of the Lakota Native American Tribe who believe that hair is sacred and a part of the spirit world.[ccl] To cut hair is bad luck which is a part of the girls' religious and cultural belief.[ccli] Immediately before and after the girls hair was cut they lost grandparents.[cclii] The school stated that the girl's hair was cut to check for lice and to keep the students at the school safe.[ccliii] The schools' officials occasionally cut the kids hair to stop the spread of lice.[ccliv] The school policy makes no mention of lice checks and the girls hair did not contain any lice.[cclv] The mother of the girls filed a lawsuit in May of 2021 citing that the girls first amendment rights were violated.[cclvi] The schools lawyers filed a motion to dismiss, citing that the school was not aware of the cultural sensitivity of cutting the girls hair.[cclvii]

Cutting a child's hair by a school official is not uncommon unfortunately. The parents of a Minnesota 12-year-old Black boy Tadow McReynolds, wanted answers after their son came home from school with his Afro cut off.[cclviii] McReynolds' parents were allowing his hair to grow out in an afro so that he could wear other hairstyles akin to African culture, when one day he came home with his hair cut.[cclix] When local social media became aware of the teacher cutting the child's hair without parental permission and without the proper hair tools, a local barber came to the rescue to cut McReynolds hair the proper way.[cclx]

A Michigan father filed a $1 Million lawsuit against his seven-year-old biracial daughter's school when she came home with her hair cut.[cclxi] Jurnee Hoffmeyer's father stated that a school official cut his daughter's hair without permission.[cclxii] The lawsuit alleges Hoffmeyer's civil rights were violated and that she faced discrimination because of her race and ethnicity.[cclxiii] In many cases, as is often in the law, these cases can settle and we will never hear about the case again because of confidentiality requirements with settlements. Therefore, the CROWN Act needs to be state and federal law so that there is no need for a settlement table. This type of behavior and discrimination by school officials should never occur and the passage of a protective law can thwart these acts.

These instances show how culturally insensitive and just unaware the majority are when it comes to cultural practices and beliefs of other members of society. The audacity of a school official to think that it is okay to cut the hair of a child that is not their own. One can imagine the outrage a parent feels when another person touches their child without permission. This is especially so for a Black child's hair. Black parents, in many cases, are forced to spend large amounts of money doing and maintaining a child's hair to ensure that their hair is well kept for school. For an administrator to take it upon themselves to alter a child's hair under the guise of a school hair policy is absurd.[cclxiv] And even more so when the hair is cut because of a policy that is racially discriminatory.

In 2022, a post was circulating on social media for Jacob A. Rush who was told by school administrators at Abeka Academy in Fort Lauderdale, FL that he could not walk in his high school graduation with his hair in locs.[cclxv] His mother made a post on her social media platform, urging followers to sign and share a petition she created to force the school to allow her son to walk in his graduation without having to cut his hair.[cclxvi] After the news of the discriminatory guidelines made waves across social media, the school apologized for the hair policy acknowledging that the guideline was insensitive.[cclxvii] However, his mother felt that the apology did not go far enough as the school had not removed the term "dreadlocks" from the guidelines.[cclxviii] The school was also requiring Rush to tuck his hair under his graduation cap.[cclxix] In late April of 2022, after the outpouring from social media and the petition reaching over 100K signatures, the school announced that Rush would be able to participate in the graduation with his hair as is.[cclxx]

Not long after this story, another video went viral on social media of a Black young lady who was competing in a state championship weightlifting competition.[cclxxi] Her teammates and coach were surrounding her working quickly to remove the beads from the Black young lady's hair so that she could compete in the competition.[cclxxii] It appeared from the video that a judge must have ruled that her hair beads did not meet the rules for competition.[cclxxiii] So, in front of everyone, the Black teen Diamond Campbell, her coach, and teammates removed the beads from her hair.[cclxxiv] Campbell said she felt shamed and humiliated about the occurrence.[cclxxv] As mentioned previously, beads in many sports, are not allowed because they pose a risk to athletes should the beads fall out. But in this case, we must ask do we blame the referee or the coach? I know it's hard to stay on top of rules, but the coach should have known about these rules and coached her athletes on proper attire, including hair beads. The bigger issue may be just the lack of understanding. It appears that most of the athletes were White, and the coach was White. The team effort to assist Campbell was great teamwork but the lack of overall understanding and the humiliation of having to change your hair in front of everyone is the ignored problem.

Public school systems enjoy a broad range of sovereign immunity. That means that a school cannot be sued for a rule, policy, practice, or occurrence unless the state has authorized that particular lawsuit to occur. If schools and school officials are operating under a law, rule, policy, or practice, getting relief from the school may be an uphill battle. If it is found that the school official is acting outside of the laws, rules, or policies, getting any type of relief can be difficult but may not be impossible. But ultimately, the school as the arbiter of the policy, goes unpunished and in many instances continue the same path unless public pressure forces them to see the error and take corrective measures. Not only do schools and school officials need to be held accountable, but there also needs to be a holistic and robust response to schools policies that are discriminatory in nature and officials that take matters into their own hands. There needs to be accountability for schools and its officials when they act in a discriminatory or culturally insensitive manner.

Brookings Institute, which is a nonprofit public policy organization based in the District of Columbia, published an article that explored steps that schools can take to combat discriminatory hair policies in the school system.[cclxxvi] The article mentioned six recommendations including: enacting moratoriums on discretionary suspensions to reduce the number of suspensions; collect data and analyze school discipline data to improve transparency and accountability; use focus groups to understand school disciplinary concerns; form a community task force to "increased family engagement, cultivated student learning, and improved attendance, behavior; and development;"[cclxxvii] implement cultural awareness training and "adopt a positive behavioral intervention and support framework which" is an "application of evidence-based prevention strategies with the use of layered scales of measures and outcomes that support student academic, emotional, social, and behavioral needs."[cclxxviii] This is a unique take on trying to stop discrimination in schools. Implementing these types of policies can help curb hair policies that are discriminatory.

The Bookings Institute article, while offering great recommendations to combat hair discrimination, makes one wonder why we must go to such extremes to prove that hair is hair. To prove that a student's hair should not be a reason that you penalize them, knowing that the penalties can follow a student forever. If we make a person's hair a normal occurrence, we will no longer have to distinguish between the differences in hairstyles, or hair textures. We will only see hair and nothing more.

A school district in Seattle, Washington has opted to create a policy that is inclusive of the diversity in their school system. The school district's new policy states that,

> "'[s]tudents should be able to dress and style their hair for school in a manner that expresses their individuality without fear of unnecessary discipline or body shaming; students have the right to be treated equitably [and] dress code enforcement will not create disparities, reinforce or increase marginalization

of any group, nor will it be more strictly enforced against students because of racial identity, ethnicity, gender identity, gender expression, gender nonconformity, sexual orientation, cultural or religious identity, household income, body size/type, or body maturity.'"[cclxxix]

The school's previous policy was not this clear and focused. The old policy left much for interpretation and bias in the administration of the policy. The school district has a race equity advancement department whose mission and vision is committed to racial equity.[cclxxx] In September of 2022, the Governor of Alaska signed a bill that would ban hair discrimination in schools.[cclxxxi] The bill also bans schools from prohibiting students from wearing "traditional regalia and other culturally significant items during school graduation ceremonies."[cclxxxii] The bill however, fell short of totally banning hair discrimination in the state.[cclxxxiii]

Laws and policies that ban hair discrimination can help curb the startling statistics that show Black girls make up 42% of school expulsions and more than a third of girls' school arrests, when they only make up 16% of the overall population in U.S. public schools.[cclxxxiv] This is believed to be due to zero tolerance school policies that leave little room for discretionary decision making for educators and administrators. The way Black students are penalized in the school system is similar to the way Black people in general are penalized in the criminal justice system. Policies that allow for Black students to be penalized at a higher rate compared to other races of students feeds into the school to prison pipeline. Black students are being punished for minor infractions such as how hair is styled and in turn being labeled as problem students. This gives the students a negative label that can follow them literally for the rest of their lives.

When I applied to law school, the questions were very broad when asking about my past. These questions specifically asked about disciplinary actions in educational settings. I cannot imagine having to explain on a college application that I was suspended from school for not following an outright discriminatory school policy that did not allow my hairstyle. It seems unbelievable that this is what we have come to, but this is the reality for many Black students across America. While this book has outlined several instances that have made news headlines, for every one instance of racism that we know of, there could be hundreds or thousands more that are not known.

With all these occurrences we must wonder why? Why are so many entities and schools starting to implement policies that blatantly discriminate against a group of students. And how are they getting away with it? It can't be that well, parents signed an agreement stating that their kids can be discriminated against, so that is the end of the conversation. Many parents are not even aware of the policies and are presented with the policies in a take it or leave it fashion, not really thinking they have a choice in the matter. Unless braids or locs are specifically mentioned in the school policies, which some schools have specifically mentioned, who really is the arbiter of what is deemed an extreme hairstyle.

This must stop, hair discrimination is real, and it is real in our schools. We have the power to make this change. Black Americans need to get involved and stay involved so that we are not excluded when policies and laws are enacted that have a direct effect on us and our kids. To ensure that these rules, policies, and procedures never make it to the light of day, there must be participation on all levels from ALL parents and members of the community. Parents need to be present in the rooms where rules and policies are being made and voted on. It should never be the case that a parent or group of parents are signing off on policies that they did not have previous involvement or planning in the process. Parents need to collectively take a stance against these policies and push for their localities to support and promote equity and inclusion for all students. It starts with awareness and involvement in the processes. The more the voices of the people who are negatively affected by these rules and policies are heard, the less likely the rule or policy maker can continue the same discriminatory path. As we have seen, once schools are faced with public backlash because of their discriminatory policies, they tend to change.

These policies can have a lifetime effect on the students that they target. In the political and social climate of America, after arguably one of the most divisive presidencies and elections in history, why is discrimination on the rise? History will tell us, but the passing of the CROWN Act can create more balance as we make amends.

APRIL MARIA WILLIAMS

Hair Discrimination Is Not Just An American Issue, But A Global Concern

We cannot ignore that hair discrimination is not just an American issue. Racism has and continues to be a global concern. In recent years we have seen how widespread the Black Lives Matter movement was and its global impact. The message that Black Lives Matter is viral and global. Ending hair discrimination is also a growing concern globally. The same focus and energy put into the Black Lives Matter Movement is needed to end hair discrimination in America and globally.

Prior to the opening of the 2020 Olympics, hair discrimination was at the forefront of those games. Alice Dearing, the first Black female swimmer on Great Britain's Olympic team made headlines when she was told that she could not wear the Soul cap at the 2020 Tokyo Summer Olympic Games.[cclxxxv] The Soul Cap is a swim cap that was invented for women with voluminous hair.[cclxxxvi] The Soul Cap has a little more room than the traditional swimming cap. The cap suits women and kids who wear traditionally Black hairstyles such as, afros, braids, twists, and locs. This swim cap has enough room to hold the hair. The swim cap has been worn by black girls all over the world who want to swim and hold their hairstyles in place. The banning of the Soul Cap sparked outrage across the globe. A petition was started on Change.org to get the Olympic officials to change the policy. The policy was seen as being another injustice that Black people have to face.[cclxxxvii] Ultimately, the Olympic committee upheld the ban on the Soul Cap, arguing that the cap was unnecessary because it ""does not follow "the natural form of the head.""[cclxxxviii] This was a reminder of how hair discrimination continues to affect ALL Black people who choose their natural hair and hairstyles akin to African culture. However, in September of 2022 the Federation Internationale de Natation or FINA the national governing body for aquatic sports walked back their decision citing that, ""[p]romoting diversity and inclusivity is at the heart of FINA's work, and it is very important that all aquatic athletes have access to the appropriate swimwear.""[cclxxxix]

  Hair discrimination is also an issue in the United Kingdom's schools and the workplace. Women across the United Kingdom are speaking out against hair discrimination. The United Kingdom's Equality Act of 2010 protects against racial discrimination, but the law does not protect against hair discrimination.[ccxc] There has been a push to end this type of discrimination in the United Kingdom through the Halo Code and through several organizations and Members of the Parliament calling for hair discrimination to be classified as a form of racism.[ccxci] The United Kingdom is different from the United States because discrimination against a person's afro is allowed. The United States views an afro as a naturally occurring hairstyle making it immutable to Black people.[ccxcii]

  Black people in the United Kingdom who face hair discrimination have virtually no legal protection. Campaigners have made calls for hair discrimination to be deemed a form of racism and are working toward ending hair discrimination.[ccxciii] The Halo Collective, which was founded by Black United Kingdom activists, strives to eradicate discrimination against afros and afro hairstyles in the United Kingdom.[ccxciv] The Halo Code is a pledge to not discriminate against afro hairstyles signed by schools and businesses.[ccxcv] Unilever United Kingdom the parent company of Dove, who supports and promotes the CROWN Act, has become the first employer to adopt the Halo Code.[ccxcvi]

In the Hair Equality Report of 2019 conducted by World Afro Day, the study found that school age children felt that their Afro hair was not understood or valued in society or in the school systems.[ccxcvii] The study involved over 1000 respondents from age groups 19-70 years old.[ccxcviii] The study was conducted to show why the United Kingdom's Afro hair needs to be protected in United Kingdom schools.[ccxcix] The study also found that school rules are increasingly promoting hair discrimination against Black and mixed-race children.[ccc] The study also found that,

> "[f]or the 1 in 6 black children [in the United Kingdom], who are having bad experiences. . . . 46% of the schools that they attend, have policies that penalize Afro hair. While attending school, nearly 82.8% are experiencing touching hair without permission, 58% are experiencing name calling or negative behavior and 59% are experiencing uncomfortable questions about their Afro-textured hair."[ccci]

This is leading to lack of self-love and self-identity in children because young children are wanting to change their appearance to look more European with a straighter hair look.[cccii] Even though the Equality Act of 2010 is supposed to curb this type of discrimination, there is a clear problem with schools that create policies that disparage Afro hair.[ccciii] The report shows that there is a need to examine schools that are continuing to discriminate against Black children in this manner.[ccciv] The report also calls for a clear message to be sent to the schools, society and its actors that they will be held to the Equality Act.[cccv] There is a general lack of awareness of how major hair discrimination is for those impacted and why it's important to enforce the laws that protect school children from this type of discrimination.[cccvi]

This study raises the question that many Black people and other minority people wonder each day about laws made to promote equality.[cccvii] When a law is enacted that grants a group of people the same protections that others already have, i.e. the right to not have your hair discriminated against, why is it so hard to enforce.[cccviii] How can a law that has been enacted almost a decade ago (the civil rights act of 1964 almost 6 decades ago in the United States), still need other research and laws to protect against the very discrimination that the law is already supposed to protect against?[cccix] Why are these protections still so hard to enforce?[cccx] The answer lies with the views of the majority and how those views have been superimposed on everyone else, so much that Black people believe that they have no choice but to conform.[cccxi] Black people fear facing the discrimination that comes with wearing their hair in its natural state and in hairstyles that can protect their natural hair.[cccxii] Not to forget how the narrow definition of race tends to exclude cultural differences.

Kids that wear braids, fades, locs, and natural afros are specifically being attacked in the United Kingdom as well.[cccxiii] In 2018, Chikayzea Flanders was told to leave the school or cut off his locs.[cccxiv] Flanders' mother launched a campaign against the school which caused the school to back track their decision.[cccxv] In 2019, Josiah Sharpe was excluded from breaktimes and was sent home because the school found that his "fade" haircut style was considered extreme.[cccxvi] "[Sharpe's] mother, who is a hairdresser, offered to come into the school and give a presentation about Afro hair but the Head Teacher refused."[cccxvii] In 2020, Ruby Williams, a student at Urswick School in east London settled a lawsuit against the school when she was told that her afro hair style violated school policy.[cccxviii] Williams was told that her natural afro hair was too big, was distracting to other students, and obscured the view of other students in the classroom.[cccxix] Imagine how a child must feel when their hair in its natural state is considered distracting. Unfortunately, there is no uniform law that bans hair discrimination in schools.

In other countries children are facing the same type of hair discrimination as children in the United Kingdom. In South Africa, Zulaikha Patel, and her peers began their 2016 campaign, Stop Racism At Pretoria Girls High, to stop hair discrimination at their formerly all-white school.[cccxx] The students protested against their school in order to shed light globally on what they were facing.[cccxxi] The story made the news nationally and showed the world how hair discrimination affects kids at the school and the extreme measures taken against students who protest against this type of discrimination.[cccxxii] Police with guns and a K-9 in tow where called to the silent student protest.[cccxxiii] The school policies have since changed but they remain very restrictive towards Black students.[cccxxiv]

As recent as July of 2022, two sisters Safhira and Amayah Row who wore their hair in braids, were suspended from Highview College in Maryborough Australia.[cccxxv] The school policy required the girls to tie their hair back to prevent pain.[cccxxvi] The girls' mother went to the school to let the school know that the policy was discriminatory but was met with backlash and seen as being overly assertive and aggressive in the defense of her children.[cccxxvii] The Principal at the school, did not acquiesce to the demand to change the culturally insensitive policy and stated that the girls "were *choosing* not to accommodate school expectations".[cccxxviii] The language of the school policy, which has since been updated, required hair to be brushed and labeled braids and locs as extreme hairstyles.[cccxxix] An educator and founder of Embrace For Every Curl, identified how having to tie back hair into a bun or ponytail can cause tension and damage to Black hair when critiquing the school policy.[cccxxx]

Black people in the United Kingdom are also experiencing

hair discrimination in the workplace. From Afros to hairstyles akin to African culture, hair discrimination is real. Lara Odoffin was offered a job that was later withdrawn because she wore her hair in braids.[cccxxxi] Odoffin's story is similar to Chasity Johnson, the pinnacle US case on hair discrimination that sparked the CROWN Act movement.[cccxxxii] The employer told Odoffin that her hair did not fit into the dress code or grooming policy and therefore could not be worn in the workplace.[cccxxxiii] For another instance, "a Black woman claimed she was told by an external agency to chemically straighten her hair if she wanted a job at the high-end department store Harrods."[cccxxxiv]

Hair Discrimination is just one means of maintaining current societal standards that caters to certain groups.[cccxxxv] While American law has been reviewed to help gain an understanding of hair discrimination, it remains a problem prevalent in America and abroad. If America passes the Crown Act, it can pave the way for similar laws in other countries. America, as world leader, should act as such by showing the world that it will not stand for hair discrimination, or any type of discrimination. The challenge for the CROWN Act, as is the case for any legislation of the magnitude, is how will it be interpreted and enforced. The good thing about the CROWN Act, in the United States, is that the law is race specific, which means, when challenged, it will be adjudged at the highest level of scrutiny, strict scrutiny. Strict scrutiny requires a showing of a compelling interest that is narrowly tailored to achieve the governmental interest. The CROWN Act is just that. With its passage, people who discriminate based on hair can finally be held accountable.

MY HAIR IS STILL PROFESSIONAL TOO! WHERE ARE WE NOW?

APRIL MARIA WILLIAMS

Black Hair On Display

In recent years, there has been an increase in inclusivity in mainstream and nonmainstream media that celebrates Black heritage through positive images of Black people with natural hair styles. In the Oscar Winning short film, Hair Love, a father tries to do his daughter's natural hair for the first time.[cccxxxvi] The show was created by Matthew A. Cherry who was inspired by seeing videos of men doing their daughter's hair.[cccxxxvii] The short film was a hit and has paved the way for more images like Hair Love to be produced.

There are other kids shows that have explored Black hair struggles. One such show is Karma's World. The show was created by rapper Ludacris, and centers on Karma, a Black middle school aged girl who wears a big beautiful curly afro.[cccxxxviii] In the episode "Hair Comes Trouble," Karma has a sleepover and her friends who do not have Afro textured hair tell her that her hair is different.[cccxxxix] Karma explores the differences in her hair compared to her friends but concludes that she also loves her hair. [cccxl]

In another animated mini-series Rise Up and Sing Out, the show touches on maintaining Black hairstyles at night.[cccxli] In the episode, Super Bonnets, Little Nia, explains why it's important for Black girls to wear a bonnet on their hair at night.[cccxlii] Other shows, Ada's Twist, Motown Magic and Esme and Roy all show Black kids with hairstyles akin to Black and African culture.[cccxliii] While there are several shows that display natural hairstyles for Black girls, there are fewer shows depicting Black boys with hairstyles akin to African culture. The boys typically have a basic afro short haircut style, but many men and boys wear braids, fades, locs and twists.

A YouTube show Grace's Corner uses song and dance routines to teach kids numbers, letters, colors, and a host of important developmental information.[cccxliv] The main character, Gracie, is a Black girl that wears an afro hair style and chants positive affirmations while lighting up the screen with vibrant music and songs. She has a song called "I love My Hair!", in which Gracie sings about loving her natural hair.[cccxlv] This song is great for teaching Black kids at a young age to love their appearance including their natural hair.

There has also been an increase in the number of Black Children's books that express hair love. The book Hair Love, discussed above is also a children's book with the same story line.[cccxlvi] Hair Story, is a book about two girls that explore ancestral roots of their hair by playing hair salon.[cccxlvii] The Coco Love Her Curly Hair book, shows kids at a young age to love their hair as well.[cccxlviii]

These are just a few. There are several books available for children to see positive images of Black children. Recently, seeing the lack of coloring books that showed Black children, I released a coloring book series: The Beauty Of Hair In Color, The Beauty Of Hair In Color: Afros, Braids, Fades and Locs, and The Beauty Of Hair In Color: Black Hair History. The response has been tremendously positive. Kids love seeing and coloring images that are representative of them and their culture.

While there has been several children's books, movies and images showing Black hair love to Black children, there has been a concerted effort to keep these books and images out of the very place where children spend most of their time, in schools. Many states have taken up legislation to keep these books along with pertinent information about Black History out of schools.[cccxlix] Critical Race Theory, a legal theory that explains how race is worked into all the systems of America, has been a major topic of discussion when it comes to the rights of parents to decide what their child should be taught.[cccl]

There is an idea that teaching things about race in school will make kids feel bad about their current identity and the past wrongs of their ancestors which opposers believe could be detrimental to a child's development. The states that have taking up or passed such legislation feel that parents should have the right to say no to information they do not want to be taught to their children. This can be seen as hypocritical, considering that these same governments will require students to learn other material that may make other kids feel bad about their racial background.

In Katy, Texas, Jerry Craft the author of the children's book New Kid, was asked not to show up for a scheduled appearance to discuss his book.[cccli] The award-winning author, talks about Black issues that Black kids face in certain school settings.[ccclii] Also, in Texas at the Little League World Series Championship, kids were caught on camera putting cotton in a little Black boy's hair.[cccliii] To think if little league kids were taught about the real struggles of people who picked cotton in America, these kids would know this is not right.

Black hair on Black women has also come full circle in showcasing beautiful Black hairstyles on main character television roles. Most recently in the HBO series Insecure, one of the main character's Molly was given the spotlight for her natural

66

hair fade short haircut.[cccliv] Molly's character is a prominent lawyer, who struggled in previous seasons trying to find herself.[ccclv] In this last season donning a slick Fade, she owns her life, career, and natural hair. This was important for the world to see that you can be Black, smart, beautiful, wear your natural hair, fit into corporate America, and still be very good in life and at your job. In another show, Our Kind of People, the series showcased Black hair on all levels.[ccclvi] Each episode gave you beautiful and exciting Black hair styles. From the simple braided hairstyles to the extravagant hairstyles, the series shows that Black hair is beautiful and comes in different textures, colors, and styles.

Bad Hair is another movie that explores Black hair in the form of a hair horror movie.[ccclvii] The storyline shows a Black woman having to alter her natural hair into a straight hair weaved hairstyle to obtain the level of success she dreamed of.[ccclviii] She turns her back on her natural hair and natural hair friends and colleagues to move up the ladder at work.[ccclix] This scenario, while in a movie, is all to familiar for Black women globally. Wear your hair the way we tell you to be appeasing and accepted in society. But as mentioned in My Hair Is Professional TOO!, we are conforming to standards that were not set by Black people nor were they made to be inclusive of Black people.[ccclx] Black people are told to conform to the standards or in many instances be left out. That of course is not right, because it minimizes the qualifications that Black people have worked so hard to obtain and continue to strive for.

Seeing positive images of yourself whether it's on the television or in a book is important. Learning about yourself is important. Living in a society that accepts you as you are, is also important. While some would say it's easy to just change to fit in, but as mentioned earlier in this book there are consequences to health and a hefty expense to maintaining hairstyles that are accepting in society. Black people are being forced to maintain a standard that does not take into consideration the damage it does to hair, health, finances, and overall quality of life. All things associated with the impacts of hair discrimination can have an impact on a person's quality of life mentally, physically, and socially. This should not be a forced decision.

APRIL MARIA WILLIAMS

What Do We Do Now To End Hair Discrimination?

With all that has been discussed, there is always the question at the end, what do we do now? How do we stop hair discrimination that continues to go on despite broad campaign messages that promote changes to policies that allow hair discrimination? We cannot let up, not for one minute! Until no one faces hair discrimination based on how your hair is styled, we must continue to do all the things that bring awareness and promotes change to this cause. Here are a few things that we can continue to do to help deter this type of discrimination.

Educate the masses about hair discrimination. When the topic of My Hair Is Professional TOO! comes up in conversations, many people of other races are just not aware of how laws and policies have been shaped to promote this type of discrimination. They are just not aware of how big of an issue hair discrimination is for those that are affected. We need to educate people about the laws and policies that promote and allow hair discrimination. My Hair Is Professional TOO!, gives a full legal analysis of the laws that have shaped hair discrimination, explains why change is needed, and how we can go about affecting change.[ccclxi] My Hair Is Still

Professional TOO!: Where Are We Now?, outlines the law that can have sweeping change moving forward, The CROWN Act. When you read the CROWN Act and see how Black people are just asking for the same treatment as others, you can understand that it is important for hair discrimination to end.

We also need to continue to educate the masses on the expense of conforming and health concerns that Black people face when trying to change their hair to fit into what is deemed professional. You should not have to choose between your health and the ability to provide for your family. If one chooses to wear chemically processed hair, it should be their decision, no one should make or force the choice on them. We can foster more compassion for those affected by hair discrimination by continuing to educate the masses. This can have the effect of pushing for an end to hair discrimination by those that have the power to do so.

Don't stop talking and sharing your stories of hair discrimination. The more stories that are shared about hair discrimination, the lengths that Black people go through to fit into society, and the effects to health and overall quality of life; the more the people who are perpetuating this discrimination can see how detrimental their discriminatory actions are. This can lead to changes in behaviors and changes in laws. When change occurs, there is, in most cases, a story behind the drive for change. If there are no stories being shared, then there is no move for change. There are people that are completely unaware of the impacts on Black people when being forced to wear hairstyles in a manner that is deemed acceptable or professional. So, keep sharing, people will see and eventually walk with you towards change.

Write to your local, state, and federal legislatures. One way to help promote change in this area is to put pressure on your elected officials to pass laws that would ban hair discrimination. You elected them and they work for you. Once election season is over, that is the opportune time to force elected officials to do the things that they promised. It is also a time to get elected officials to see how they can help impact the people they serve in a positive way. Tell your elected officials about how hair discrimination impacts you. Tell them why passing the CROWN Act is important to you or the people you know, love and support.

Implement checks and balances to ensure that hair discrimination does not happen in places where laws have been passed prohibiting hair discrimination. A mode or method of enforcement is needed that constantly checks to ensure compliance with the law. We would not want employers, schools, and people in general internalizing hair discrimination. At some point bias that are not verbalized or displayed need to be checked. That is something that laws that prohibit discrimination, at times, do not account for but is absolutely needed to maintain balance. If it looks, feels and smells of discrimination, it probably is even when done implicitly. The law must be enforced.

When considering how to enforce the CROWN Act it must be stated that laws meant to protect against discrimination are at times ill equipped with enforcement tools. The laws have been crafted in a manner that leaves it up to the individual to enforce the nondiscriminatory law that does not adequately address consequences for speaking out which often comes back to the discriminated in the form of retaliation.[ccclxii] The lack of balance in power in these situations makes it hard for the person that is being discriminated against to enforce their rights. In work settings employers use contractual agreements with "forced arbitration clauses and nondisclosure agreements that strip away employee rights and undermine effective enforcement."[ccclxiii] Even with Title VII in place to protect our most vulnerable workers, businesses are increasingly using independent contractors which enhances employers' power by creating barriers to legal recourse for discrimination.[ccclxiv]

The same can be said for children in school settings who are faced with a similar dynamic as the workplace. The students are in school districts that create discriminatory policies and student handbooks that do not allow students to wear certain hairstyles. Parents are required to sign off on a policy for their child to attend school. If a parent or child does not comply, sometimes it's not as simple as switching a child's school or home schooling the child. Some parents just don't have that option, so they are forced to comply with discriminatory policies. For the parents that can switch their child's school it does not come with ease as mentioned in previous chapters. No school is allowed to discriminate based on race, but we find ourselves here with race-based discrimination against kids and no accountability for school administrators that make and implement these policies.

While passing a law that bans hair discrimination is highly important, we also must craft policies that have real checks and balances to ensure the law is being followed and not contravened by crafty actors that want to thwart the law to retain the status quote. Whether in the workplace or at the school or just in general, we must work to ensure that hair discrimination is banned and enforced.

Finally, we must work together and fight for those that are still impacted even if you are protected. As mentioned, the CROWN Act is not the law in most of the states in the United States. And there are no laws abroad that provide for protection against hair discrimination. To eradicate hair discrimination, everyone must continue to fight until no one is impacted by this type of discrimination. A recent Facebook post highlighted hair discrimination against nurses who wore the "messy bun" hairstyle.[ccclxv] Many of the comments were like those made by Black people who do not have protection when they wear their natural hair textures and hairstyles akin to African culture.[ccclxvi] We must learn to have empathy for people facing discrimination because it does not feel good when the shoe is on the other foot. Your privilege of protection should be the driving force that leads you to want the same protections for others. Equality can only be achieved if there is equality for everyone.[ccclxvii]

As mentioned in My Hair Is Professional TOO!, the black hair industry is a $2 billion a year industry. It's an industry that is largely not owned by the very people that it serves. A study conducted by the Beauty Supply Industry found that only 3% of beauty supply stores were owned by Black people.[ccclxviii] A simple walk down beauty aisles will reveal the disparity in the cost of products marketed to Black people verses those that are marketed to others. Not to mention a study that found the products that are marketed toward Black women are known to have cancer causing ingredients.[ccclxix] Black people, men, women, and children are expected to present themselves in a certain manner to conform to what society says we are supposed to look like, but no one is looking at the cost or the time spent conforming.

Anytime a person, entity, company, or institution tells a Black person how they should look, they are telling them that their culture, health, and/or financial struggles do not matter. Conform or be left out! If we are made to conform in manners that are detrimental to a Black person, we can never have true equality with our counterparts because the things that are important to us as a matter of quality of life don't matter. Black people in all areas are penalized for not conforming to laws, policies and personal preferences that are discriminatory on its face and in practice. The 2020 census revealed that America is more diverse than it has been in the past.[ccclxx] As we become more diverse, our country is going to have to continue to move towards being more accepting of the diversity that makes up our society.

End Hair Discrimination, Pass The CROWN Act!!

APRIL MARIA WILLIAMS

Citations (*Written in accordance with the 20th Edition Bluebook*)

[i] Andrew Schneider, Meet 'Black Girl Magic,' The 19 African-American Women Elected As Judges In Texas, www.npr.com, (Jan. 16, 2019), https://www.npr.org/2019/01/16/685815783/meet-black-girl-magic-the-19-african-american-women-elected-as-judges-in-texas

[ii] About, Crown Coalition, www.thecrownact.com, https://www.thecrownact.com/about (Last visited July 5, 2022); *Virginia Langmaid, Massachusetts becomes latest state to ban discrimination based on natural hairstyles*, www.cnn.com, (July 26, 2022), https://www.cnn.com/2022/07/26/us/massachusetts-crown-act-law-hair-discrimination-reaj/index.html; *see Patrice Peck, How to Persuade White Lawmakers to Protect Black Hairstyles*, www.bloomberg.com, (Oct. 13, 2021), https://www.bloomberg.com/news/features/2021-10-13/how-to-persuade-lawmakers-to-protect-against-black-hairstyle-discrimination.

[iii] *See* April Maria Williams, Esq., My Hair Is Professional TOO!, Jumptime Publishing (2020).

[iv] *See* April Maria Williams, Esq., My Hair Is Professional TOO!, Jumptime Publishing (2020).

[v] *See* April Maria Williams, Esq., My Hair Is Professional TOO!, Jumptime Publishing (2020).

[vi] *See* April Maria Williams, Esq., My Hair Is Professional TOO!, Jumptime Publishing (2020).

[vii] *See* April Maria Williams, Esq., My Hair Is Professional TOO!, Jumptime Publishing (2020).

[viii] 29 CFR § 1607.11

[ix] 29 CFR § 1607.11

[x] 41 CFR § 60-20.2

[xi] EEOC v. Joe's Stone Crab, Inc., 220 F.3d 1263, 1268 (11th Cir. Fla. 2000); *See* April Maria Williams, Esq., My Hair Is Professional TOO!, Jumptime Publishing (2020).

[xii] EEOC v. Catastrophe Mgmt. Solutions, 852 F.3d 1018 (11th Cir. 2016); *See* April Maria Williams, Esq., My Hair Is Professional TOO!, Jumptime Publishing (2020).

[xiii] EEOC v. Catastrophe Mgmt. Solutions, 852 F.3d 1018 (11th Cir. 2016); *See* April Maria Williams, Esq., My Hair Is Professional TOO!, Jumptime Publishing (2020).

[xiv] EEOC v. Catastrophe Mgmt. Solutions, 852 F.3d 1018 (11th Cir. 2016); *See* April Maria Williams, Esq., My Hair Is Professional TOO!, Jumptime Publishing (2020).

[xv] S EEOC v. Catastrophe Mgmt. Solutions, 852 F.3d 1018 (11th Cir. 2016); *See* April Maria Williams, Esq., My Hair Is Professional TOO!, Jumptime Publishing (2020).

[xvi] EEOC v. Catastrophe Mgmt. Solutions, 852 F.3d 1018 (11th Cir. 2016); *See* April Maria Williams, Esq., My Hair Is Professional TOO!, Jumptime Publishing (2020).

[xvii] EEOC v. Catastrophe Mgmt. Solutions, 852 F.3d 1018 (11th Cir. 2016); *See* April Maria Williams, Esq., My Hair Is Professional TOO!, Jumptime Publishing (2020).

[xviii] EEOC v. Catastrophe Mgmt. Solutions, 852 F.3d 1018 (11th Cir. 2016); *See* April Maria Williams, Esq., My Hair Is Professional TOO!, Jumptime Publishing (2020).

[xix] EEOC v. Catastrophe Mgmt. Solutions, 852 F.3d 1018 (11th Cir. 2016); *See* April Maria Williams, Esq., My Hair Is Professional TOO!, Jumptime Publishing (2020).

[xx] EEOC v. Catastrophe Mgmt. Solutions, 852 F.3d 1018 (11th Cir. 2016); *See* April Maria Williams, Esq., My Hair Is Professional TOO!, Jumptime Publishing (2020).

[xxi] EEOC v. Catastrophe Mgmt. Solutions, 852 F.3d 1018 (11th Cir. 2016); *See* April Maria Williams, Esq., My Hair Is Professional TOO!, Jumptime Publishing (2020).

[xxii] A Black person's natural hair can naturally form into a loc. Locs are a type of hairstyle akin to African culture that can face hair discrimination.

[xxiii] The CROWN Act of 2020, H.R. 5309, 116th Cong. (2019); Govtrack, H.R. 5309 (116th): CROWN Act of 2020, govtrack.us, https://www.govtrack.us/congress/bills/116/hr5309 (last visited Sept. 5, 2022).

[xxiv] The CROWN Act of 2020, H.R. 5309, 116th Cong. (2019); Govtrack, H.R. 5309 (116th): CROWN Act of 2020, govtrack.us, https://www.govtrack.us/

[xxv] The CROWN Act of 2020, H.R. 5309, 116th Cong. (2019); Govtrack, H.R. 5309 (116th): CROWN Act of 2020, govtrack.us, https://www.govtrack.us/congress/bills/116/hr5309 (last visited Sept. 5, 2022).

[xxvi] The CROWN Act of 2020, S.B. 3167, 116th Cong. (2019-2020); *see generally About, CROWN Coalition*, https://www.thecrownact.com/about (last visited July. 23, 2022).

[xxvii] CROWN Act of 2021 H.R. 2116, 117th Congress (2021-2022), https://www.congress.gov/bill/117th-congress/house-bill/2116/text; CROWN Act of 2021 S.B. 888, 117th Congress (2021-2022).

[xxviii] *About, CROWN Coalition*, https://www.thecrownact.com/about (last visited Sept. 24, 2022); Virginia Langmaid, *Massachusetts becomes latest state to ban discrimination based on natural hairstyles*, www.cnn.com, (July 26, 2022), https://www.cnn.com/2022/07/26/us/massachusetts-crown-act-law-hair-discrimination-reaj/index.html; *see* Patrice Peck, *How to Persuade White Lawmakers to Protect Black Hairstyles*, www.bloomberg.com, (Oct. 13, 2021), https://www.bloomberg.com/news/features/2021-10-13/how-to-persuade-lawmakers-to-protect-against-black-hairstyle-discrimination.

[xxix] Patrice Peck, *How to Persuade White Lawmakers to Protect Black Hairstyles*, www.bloomberg.com, (Oct. 13, 2021), https://www.bloomberg.com/news/features/2021-10-13/how-to-persuade-lawmakers-to-protect-against-black-hairstyle-discrimination.

[xxx] *About, CROWN Coalition*, https://www.thecrownact.com/about (last visited July. 23, 2022).

[xxxi] Defender News Service, *Harris Co Commissioners Court approves CROWN Act resolution*, (Oct. 14, 2021), defendernetwork.com, https://defendernetwork.com/news/local-state/harris-co-commissioners-court-approves-crown-act-resolution/.

[xxxii] Candice Norwood, *A yearslong push to ban hair discrimination is gaining momentum*, pbs.org, (Mar. 30, 2021), https://www.pbs.org/newshour/politics/a-yearslong-push-to-ban-hair-discrimination-is-gaining-momentum.

[xxxiii] CROWN Act of 2021 H.R. 2116, 117th Congress (2021-2022), https://www.congress.gov/bill/117th-congress/house-bill/2116/text.

[xxxiv] CROWN Act of 2021 H.R. 2116, 117th Congress (2021-2022), https://www.congress.gov/bill/117th-congress/house-bill/2116/text.

[xxxv] CROWN Act of 2021 H.R. 2116, 117th Congress (2021-2022), https://www.congress.gov/bill/117th-congress/house-bill/2116/text

[xxxvi] April Maria Williams, Esq., My Hair Is Professional TOO!, Jumptime Publishing, p. 23-29 (2020).

[xxxvii] April Maria Williams, Esq., My Hair Is Professional TOO!, Jumptime Publishing, p. 24-25 (2020).

[xxxviii] Creating a Respectful and Open World for Natural Hair Act of 2022, H.R.

2116, 117th Cong. (2021-2022).

[xxxix] Creating a Respectful and Open World for Natural Hair Act of 2022, H.R. 2116, 117th Cong. (2021-2022).

[xl] Creating a Respectful and Open World for Natural Hair Act of 2022, H.R. 2116, 117th Cong. (2021-2022).

[xli] Creating a Respectful and Open World for Natural Hair Act of 2022, H.R. 2116, 117th Cong. (2021-2022).

[xlii] Creating a Respectful and Open World for Natural Hair Act of 2022, H.R. 2116, 117th Cong. (2021-2022).

[xliii] Creating a Respectful and Open World for Natural Hair Act of 2022, H.R. 2116, 117th Cong. (2021-2022).

[xliv] Houston Fibroids, *There's Hidden Danger in Black Hair Relaxers*, houstonfibroids.com, https://houstonfibroids.com/posts/fibroid-symptoms/warning-your-hair-products-could-be-hurting-you/, (last visited Oct. 3, 2022).

[xlv] Houston Fibroids, *There's Hidden Danger in Black Hair Relaxers*, houstonfibroids.com, https://houstonfibroids.com/posts/fibroid-symptoms/warning-your-hair-products-could-be-hurting-you/, (last visited Oct. 3, 2022); *Carolyn E. Eberle, et. al., Hair dye and chemical straightener use and breast cancer risk in a large US population of black and white women*, pubmed.ncbi.nlm.nih.gov, (July 15, 2020), https://pubmed.ncbi.nlm.nih.gov/31797377/.

[xlvi] Houston Fibroids, *There's Hidden Danger in Black Hair Relaxers*, houstonfibroids.com, https://houstonfibroids.com/posts/fibroid-symptoms/warning-your-hair-products-could-be-hurting-you/, (last visited Oct. 3, 2022); *Carolyn E. Eberle, et. al., Hair dye and chemical straightener use and breast cancer risk in a large US population of black and white women*, pubmed.ncbi.nlm.nih.gov, (July 15, 2020), https://pubmed.ncbi.nlm.nih.gov/31797377/.

[xlvii] Houston Fibroids, *There's Hidden Danger in Black Hair Relaxers*, houstonfibroids.com, https://houstonfibroids.com/posts/fibroid-symptoms/warning-your-hair-products-could-be-hurting-you/, (last visited Oct. 3, 2022); *Carolyn E. Eberle, et. al., Hair dye and chemical straightener use and breast cancer risk in a large US population of black and white women*, pubmed.ncbi.nlm.nih.gov, (July 15, 2020), https://pubmed.ncbi.nlm.nih.gov/31797377/.

[xlviii] Houston Fibroids, *There's Hidden Danger in Black Hair Relaxers*, houstonfibroids.com, https://houstonfibroids.com/posts/fibroid-symptoms/warning-your-hair-products-could-be-hurting-you/, (last visited Oct. 3, 2022).

[xlix] *Hilda Hutcherson, Black Women Are Hit Hardest by Fibroid Tumors*, nytime.com, (April 15, 2020), https://www.nytimes.com/2020/04/15/parenting/fertility/black-women-uterine-fibroids.html; see generally *Uterine fibroids*, mayoclinic.org, https://www.mayoclinic.org/diseases-conditions/uterine-fibroids/symptoms-causes/syc-20354288 (last visited Sept 5, 2022).

[l] *Hilda Hutcherson, Black Women Are Hit Hardest by Fibroid Tumors*, nytime.com, (April 15, 2020), https://www.nytimes.com/2020/04/15/parenting/fertility/black-women-uterine-fibroids.html.

[li] Houston Fibroids, *There's Hidden Danger in Black Hair Relaxers*, houstonfibroids.com, https://houstonfibroids.com/posts/fibroid-symptoms/warning-your-hair-products-could-be-hurting-you/, (last visited Oct. 3, 2022); see Hilda Hutcherson, *Black Women Are Hit Hardest by Fibroid Tumors*, nytime.com, (April 15, 2020), https://www.nytimes.com/2020/04/15/parenting/fertility/black-women-uterine-fibroids.html.

[lii] Hilda Hutcherson, *Black Women Are Hit Hardest by Fibroid Tumors*, nytime.com, (April 15, 2020), https://www.nytimes.com/2020/04/15/parenting/fertility/black-women-uterine-fibroids.html.

[liii] Houston Fibroids, *There's Hidden Danger in Black Hair Relaxers*, houstonfibroids.com, https://houstonfibroids.com/posts/fibroid-symptoms/warning-your-hair-products-could-be-hurting-you/, (last visited Oct. 3, 2022); see Hilda Hutcherson, *Black Women Are Hit Hardest by Fibroid Tumors*, nytime.com, (April 15, 2020), https://www.nytimes.com/2020/04/15/parenting/fertility/black-women-uterine-fibroids.html.

[liv] Houston Fibroids, *There's Hidden Danger in Black Hair Relaxers*, houstonfibroids.com, https://houstonfibroids.com/posts/fibroid-symptoms/warning-your-hair-products-could-be-hurting-you/, (last visited Oct. 3, 2022); see Hilda Hutcherson, *Black Women Are Hit Hardest by Fibroid Tumors*, nytime.com, (April 15, 2020), https://www.nytimes.com/2020/04/15/parenting/fertility/black-women-uterine-fibroids.html.

[lv] Houston Fibroids, *There's Hidden Danger in Black Hair Relaxers*, houstonfibroids.com, https://houstonfibroids.com/posts/fibroid-symptoms/warning-your-hair-products-could-be-hurting-you/, (last visited Oct. 3, 2022); see Hilda Hutcherson, *Black Women Are Hit Hardest by Fibroid Tumors*, nytime.com, (April 15, 2020), https://www.nytimes.com/2020/04/15/parenting/fertility/black-women-uterine-fibroids.html.

[lvi] Houston Fibroids, *There's Hidden Danger in Black Hair Relaxers*, houstonfibroids.com, https://houstonfibroids.com/posts/fibroid-symptoms/warning-your-hair-products-could-be-hurting-you/, (last visited Oct. 3, 2022); see Hilda Hutcherson, *Black Women Are Hit Hardest by Fibroid Tumors*, nytime.com, (April 15, 2020), https://www.nytimes.com/2020/04/15/parenting/fertility/black-women-uterine-fibroids.html.

[lvii] Houston Fibroids, *There's Hidden Danger in Black Hair Relaxers*, houstonfibroids.com, https://houstonfibroids.com/posts/fibroid-symptoms/warning-your-hair-products-could-be-hurting-you/, (last visited Oct. 3, 2022).

[lviii] Denver Fibroids, *How Your Hair Treatment May Impact Your Uterine Fibroids*, denverfibroids.com, https://denverfibroids.com/posts/fibroids/how-your-hair-treatment-may-impact-your-uterine-fibroids/ (last visited March 16, 2021).

[lix] Denver Fibroids, *How Your Hair Treatment May Impact Your Uterine Fibroids*, denverfibroids.com, https://denverfibroids.com/posts/fibroids/how-your-hair-treatment-may-impact-your-uterine-fibroids/ (last visited March 16, 2021).

[lx] Denver Fibroids, *How Your Hair Treatment May Impact Your Uterine Fibroids*,

denverfibroids.com, https://denverfibroids.com/posts/fibroids/how-your-hair-treatment-may-impact-your-uterine-fibroids/ (last visited March 16, 2021).

[lxi] Tayo Bero, *Black women's hair products are killing us. Why isn't more being done?*, www.theguardian.com, (July 27, 2021) https://www.theguardian.com/commentisfree/2021/jul/27/black-women-hair-products-health-hazards-study; Carolyn E. Eberle, et. al., *Hair dye and chemical straightener use and breast cancer risk in a large US population of black and white women*, onlinelibrary.wiley.com, (Dec. 3, 2019), https://onlinelibrary.wiley.com/doi/full/10.1002/ijc.32738.

[lxii] See Tayo Bero, *Black women's hair products are killing us. Why isn't more being done?*, www.theguardian.com, (July 27, 2021) https://www.theguardian.com/commentisfree/2021/jul/27/black-women-hair-products-health-hazards-study; Environmental Working Group, *Big Market for Black Cosmetics, but Less-Hazardous Choices Limited*, (Dec. 6, 2016), https://www.ewg.org/research/big-market-black-cosmetics-less-hazardous-choices-limited.

[lxiii] See Tayo Bero, *Black women's hair products are killing us. Why isn't more being done?*, www.theguardian.com, (July 27, 2021) https://www.theguardian.com/commentisfree/2021/jul/27/black-women-hair-products-health-hazards-study; Environmental Working Group, *Big Market for Black Cosmetics, but Less-Hazardous Choices Limited*, (Dec. 6, 2016), https://www.ewg.org/research/big-market-black-cosmetics-less-hazardous-choices-limited.

[lxiv] Erin Quinn, *Why The FDA Has Never Looked At Some Of The Additives In Our Food*, www.npr.org, (Apr. 14, 2015), https://www.npr.org/sections/thesalt/2015/04/14/399591292/why-the-fda-is-clueless-about-some-of-the-additives-in-our-food; Olivia Backhaus & Melanie Benesh, *EWG analysis: Almost all new food chemicals greenlighted by industry, not the FDA*, www.ewg.org, (Apr. 13, 2022), https://www.ewg.org/news-insights/news/2022/04/ewg-analysis-almost-all-new-food-chemicals-greenlighted-industry-not-fda; Claire McCarthy, MD, *Common food additives and chemicals harmful to children*, www.health.harvard.edu, (July 26, 2021), https://www.health.harvard.edu/blog/common-food-additives-and-chemicals-harmful-to-children-2018072414326.

[lxv] Erin Quinn, *Why The FDA Has Never Looked At Some Of The Additives In Our Food*, www.npr.org, (Apr. 14, 2015), https://www.npr.org/sections/thesalt/2015/04/14/399591292/why-the-fda-is-clueless-about-some-of-the-additives-in-our-food; Olivia Backhaus & Melanie Benesh, *EWG analysis: Almost all new food chemicals greenlighted by industry, not the FDA*, www.ewg.org, (Apr. 13, 2022), https://www.ewg.org/news-insights/news/2022/04/ewg-analysis-almost-all-new-food-chemicals-greenlighted-industry-not-fda; Claire McCarthy, MD, *Common food additives and chemicals harmful to children*, www.health.harvard.edu, (July 26, 2021), https://www.health.harvard.edu/blog/common-food-additives-and-chemicals-harmful-to-

children-2018072414326; *see* U.S. Food & Drug Administration, www.fda.gov, *How U.S. FDA's GRAS Notification Program Works*, https://www.fda.gov/food/generally-recognized-safe-gras/how-us-fdas-gras-notification-program-works#authors (last visited Sept. 11, 2022).

[lxvi] Erin Quinn, *Why The FDA Has Never Looked At Some Of The Additives In Our Food*, www.npr.org, (Apr. 14, 2015), https://www.npr.org/sections/thesalt/2015/04/14/399591292/why-the-fda-is-clueless-about-some-of-the-additives-in-our-food; Olivia Backhaus & Melanie Benesh, *EWG analysis: Almost all new food chemicals greenlighted by industry, not the FDA*, www.ewg.org, (Apr. 13, 2022), https://www.ewg.org/news-insights/news/2022/04/ewg-analysis-almost-all-new-food-chemicals-greenlighted-industry-not-fda; Claire McCarthy, MD, *Common food additives and chemicals harmful to children*, www.health.harvard.edu, (July 26, 2021), https://www.health.harvard.edu/blog/common-food-additives-and-chemicals-harmful-to-children-2018072414326; EWG, *Food Additives State of the Science*, www.ewg.org, https://www.ewg.org/research/food-additive-science (last visited Sept 11, 2022); U.S. Food & Drug Administration, *Is It Really 'FDA Approved'?*, www.fda.org, https://www.fda.gov/consumers/consumer-updates/it-really-fda-approved (last visited Sept. 11, 2022).

[lxvii] *See* Denver Fibroids, *How Your Hair Treatment May Impact Your Uterine Fibroids*, denverfibroids.com, https://denverfibroids.com/posts/fibroids/how-your-hair-treatment-may-impact-your-uterine-fibroids/ (last visited March 16, 2021); Erin Quinn, *Why The FDA Has Never Looked At Some Of The Additives In Our Food*, www.npr.org, (Apr. 14, 2015), https://www.npr.org/sections/thesalt/2015/04/14/399591292/why-the-fda-is-clueless-about-some-of-the-additives-in-our-food; Olivia Backhaus & Melanie Benesh, *EWG analysis: Almost all new food chemicals greenlighted by industry, not the FDA*, www.ewg.org, (Apr. 13, 2022), https://www.ewg.org/news-insights/news/2022/04/ewg-analysis-almost-all-new-food-chemicals-greenlighted-industry-not-fda; Claire McCarthy, MD, *Common food additives and chemicals harmful to children*, www.health.harvard.edu, (July 26, 2021), https://www.health.harvard.edu/blog/common-food-additives-and-chemicals-harmful-to-children-2018072414326; EWG, *Food Additives State of the Science*, www.ewg.org, https://www.ewg.org/research/food-additive-science (last visited Sept 11, 2022); U.S. Food & Drug Administration, *Is It Really 'FDA Approved'?*, www.fda.org, https://www.fda.gov/consumers/consumer-updates/it-really-fda-approved (last visited Sept. 11, 2022).

[lxviii] The FDA does not approve cosmetics. *Is It Really 'FDA Approved'?*, www.fda.org, https://www.fda.gov/consumers/consumer-updates/it-really-fda-approved (last visited Sept. 11, 2022).

[lxix] *Is It Really 'FDA Approved'?*, www.fda.org, https://www.fda.gov/consumers/consumer-updates/it-really-fda-approved (last visited Sept. 11, 2022).

[lxx] *See Not So Pretty* (HBO Max 2022); U.S. Food & Drug Administration, *Is It Really 'FDA Approved'?*, www.fda.org, https://www.fda.gov/consumers/

consumer-updates/it-really-fda-approved (last visited Sept. 11, 2022); *Erin Quinn, Why The FDA Has Never Looked At Some Of The Additives In Our Food*, www.npr.org, (Apr. 14, 2015), https://www.npr.org/sections/thesalt/2015/04/14/399591292/why-the-fda-is-clueless-about-some-of-the-additives-in-our-food; *Olivia Backhaus & Melanie Benesh, EWG analysis: Almost all new food chemicals greenlighted by industry, not the FDA*, www.ewg.org, (Apr. 13, 2022), https://www.ewg.org/news-insights/news/2022/04/ewg-analysis-almost-all-new-food-chemicals-greenlighted-industry-not-fda; Claire McCarthy, MD, *Common food additives and chemicals harmful to children*, www.health.harvard.edu, (July 26, 2021), https://www.health.harvard.edu/blog/common-food-additives-and-chemicals-harmful-to-children-2018072414326; EWG, *Food Additives State of the Science*, www.ewg.org, https://www.ewg.org/research/food-additive-science (last visited Sept 11, 2022); U.S. Food & Drug Administration, *Is It Really 'FDA Approved'?*, www.fda.org, https://www.fda.gov/consumers/consumer-updates/it-really-fda-approved (last visited Sept. 11, 2022).

[lxxi] Allana Akhtar, *A toxic chemical used in hair products for Black women can fuel breast cancer, study finds*, (June 13, 2022), https://www.insider.com/toxic-chemical-spreads-cancer-hair-products-for-black-women-2022-6?utm_source=clubhouse; Letisia Marquez, Chemicals in personal care products cause harmful effects in breast cancer cells from Black women, www.cityofhope.org, (June 14, 2022), https://www.cityofhope.org/chemicals-cause-harmful-effects-black-women; *See* Bench To Community Home, bench2community.org, https://www.bench2community.org (last visited June 30, 2022).

[lxxii] Allana Akhtar, A toxic chemical used in hair products for Black women can fuel breast cancer, study finds, (June 13, 2022), https://www.insider.com/toxic-chemical-spreads-cancer-hair-products-for-black-women-2022-6?utm_source=clubhouse; Letisia Marquez, Chemicals in personal care products cause harmful effects in breast cancer cells from Black women, www.cityofhope.org, (June 14, 2022), https://www.cityofhope.org/chemicals-cause-harmful-effects-black-women; *See* Bench To Community Home, bench2community.org, https://www.bench2community.org (last visited June 30, 2022).

[lxxiii] Letisia Marquez, Chemicals in personal care products cause harmful effects in breast cancer cells from Black women, www.cityofhope.org, (June 14, 2022), https://www.cityofhope.org/chemicals-cause-harmful-effects-black-women.

[lxxiv] Allana Akhtar, A toxic chemical used in hair products for Black women can fuel breast cancer, study finds, (June 13, 2022), https://www.insider.com/toxic-chemical-spreads-cancer-hair-products-for-black-women-2022-6?utm_source=clubhouse; Letisia Marquez, Chemicals in personal care products cause harmful effects in breast cancer cells from Black women, www.cityofhope.org, (June 14, 2022), https://www.cityofhope.org/chemicals-

cause-harmful-effects-black-women; *See* Bench To Community Home, bench2community.org, https://www.bench2community.org (last visited June 30, 2022).

[lxxv] *See Center for Disease Control and Prevention, What is breast cancer?*, www.cdc.gov, https://www.cdc.gov/cancer/breast/basic_info/screening.htm (last visited June 30, 2022); *see American Cancer Society, American Cancer Society Guidelines for the Early Detection of Cancer*, www.cancer.org, https://www.cancer.org/healthy/find-cancer-early/american-cancer-society-guidelines-for-the-early-detection-of-cancer.html (last visited June 30, 2022).

[lxxvi] American Academy of Family Physicians Foundation, *Minorities Are Underrepresented in Clinical Trials*, www.aafp.org, https://www.aafp.org/news/blogs/leadervoices/entry/20181204lv-clinicaltrials.html (last visited Sept. 11, 2022).

[lxxvii] Letisia Marquez, Chemicals in personal care products cause harmful effects in breast cancer cells from Black women, www.cityofhope.org, (June 14, 2022), https://www.cityofhope.org/chemicals-cause-harmful-effects-black-women.

[lxxviii] Che-Jung Chang, PhD, et. al., *Use of Straighteners and Other Hair Products and Incident Uterine Cancer*, academic.oup.com, Oct. 17, 2022, https://academic.oup.com/jnci/advance-article/doi/10.1093/jnci/djac165/6759686?searchresult=1; Char Adams, *Chemical hair straighteners linked to higher risk of uterine cancer for Black women, study shows*, www.nbcnews.com, (Oct. 19, 2022), https://www.nbcnews.com/news/amp/rcna52576?fbclid=IwAR0o4Dn4iVeKOLfE_2U1hQMVlYu8DB5f56nXORbl4_S0ELhagaQbwXPF7mI.

[lxxix] Che-Jung Chang, PhD, et. al., *Use of Straighteners and Other Hair Products and Incident Uterine Cancer*, academic.oup.com, Oct. 17, 2022, https://academic.oup.com/jnci/advance-article/doi/10.1093/jnci/djac165/6759686?searchresult=1; Char Adams, *Chemical hair straighteners linked to higher risk of uterine cancer for Black women, study shows*, www.nbcnews.com, (Oct. 19, 2022), https://www.nbcnews.com/news/amp/rcna52576?fbclid=IwAR0o4Dn4iVeKOLfE_2U1hQMVlYu8DB5f56nXORbl4_S0ELhagaQbwXPF7mI.

[lxxx] Che-Jung Chang, PhD, et. al., *Use of Straighteners and Other Hair Products and Incident Uterine Cancer*, academic.oup.com, Oct. 17, 2022, https://academic.oup.com/jnci/advance-article/doi/10.1093/jnci/djac165/6759686?searchresult=1; Char Adams, *Chemical hair straighteners linked to higher risk of uterine cancer for Black women, study shows*, www.nbcnews.com, (Oct. 19, 2022), https://www.nbcnews.com/news/amp/rcna52576?fbclid=IwAR0o4Dn4iVeKOLfE_2U1hQMVlYu8DB5f56nXORbl4_S0ELhagaQbwXPF7mI; *see* Letisia Marquez, Chemicals in personal care products cause harmful effects in breast cancer cells from Black women, www.cityofhope.org, (June 14, 2022), https://www.cityofhope.org/chemicals-cause-harmful-

effects-black-women.

[lxxxi] *See Che-Jung Chang, PhD, et. al., Use of Straighteners and Other Hair Products and Incident Uterine Cancer*, academic.oup.com, Oct. 17, 2022, https://academic.oup.com/jnci/advance-article/doi/10.1093/jnci/djac165/6759686?searchresult=1.

[lxxxii] *Che-Jung Chang, PhD, et. al., Use of Straighteners and Other Hair Products and Incident Uterine Cancer*, academic.oup.com, Oct. 17, 2022, https://academic.oup.com/jnci/advance-article/doi/10.1093/jnci/djac165/6759686?searchresult=1; *Char Adams, Chemical hair straighteners linked to higher risk of uterine cancer for Black women, study shows*, www.nbcnews.com, (Oct. 19, 2022), https://www.nbcnews.com/news/amp/rcna52576?fbclid=IwAR0o4Dn4iVeKOLfE_2U1hQMVlYu8DB5f56nXORbl4_S0ELhagaQbwXPF7mI.

[lxxxiii] *Megan Leonhardt, Consumers can't sue some of the biggest companies in the US—here's what that means for you*, www.cnbc.com, (July 12 2019), https://www.cnbc.com/2019/07/12/why-you-cant-sue-fortune-100-companies.html

[lxxxiv] This article shows that Johnson & Johnson knew for a very long time that it's baby powder products poses risk to a person's health, but they continued to sell the product. *see Lisa Girion, Johnson & Johnson knew for decades that asbestos lurked in its Baby Powder A Reuters Investigation*, www.reuters.com, (Dec. 14, 2018), https://www.reuters.com/investigates/special-report/johnsonandjohnson-cancer/; *see also* Not So Pretty (HBO Max 2022).

[lxxxv] *See Kori Hale, Johnson & Johnson Attempts To Side-Step $100 Million Baby Powder Settlement*, www.forbes.com, (Mar. 2, 2022), https://www.forbes.com/sites/korihale/2022/03/02/johnson--johnson-attempts-to-side-step-100-million-baby-powder-settlement/?sh=5fe4e43947ef; *see also Geoff Mulvihill, Appeals court to consider paving way for Purdue Pharma deal out of bankruptcy*, www.pbs.org, (Apr. 29, 2022), https://www.pbs.org/newshour/nation/appeals-court-to-consider-paving-way-for-purdue-pharma-deal-out-of-bankruptcy.

[lxxxvi] *Oliver Milman, US cosmetics are full of chemicals banned by Europe – why?*, amp.theguardian.com, (May 22, 2019), https://amp.theguardian.com/us-news/2019/may/22/chemicals-in-cosmetics-us-restricted-eu.

[lxxxvii] Breast Cancer Prevention Partners, *New Federal Bill Package Will Make Safer Beauty Available to All*, (July 29, 2021), https://www.bcpp.org/resource/new-federal-bill-package-will-make-safer-beauty-available-to-all/.

[lxxxviii] *see* Cal. Cosmetic Fragrance and Flavor Ingredient Right to Know Act (CFFIRKA); *see also* California Department of Health, California Safe Cosmetic Program, Ch. 315, Sec. 3. (SB 312) (2020); https://www.cdph.ca.gov/Programs/CCDPHP/DEODC/OHB/CSCP/Pages/CSCP.aspx?
TSPD_101_R0=087ed344cfab20006719f77753ad725f322c94deb52e3ac704a343f0c8fd24ee76e6f526f2603e6808b68ef53a143000e501191ce239a9670b056a67aa630a5cd78101583d9438805fd734c9b82028632c9d725afd6903da150

f26ef1814eca4 (last visited Sept. 11, 2022).

[lxxxix] *Tamara E. Holmes, Feature: The Industry That Black Women Built*, www.essence.com, (Dec. 6, 2020), https://www.essence.com/news/money-career/business-black-beauty/.

[xc] *Ruth Etiesit Samuel, The Little Black Girls We Adored On Relaxer Boxes Are Going Viral On Twitter*, www.huffpost.com, (Oct.4, 2022), https://www.huffpost.com/entry/black-girls-relaxer-boxes-going-viral_n_633c8ee2e4b03e8038c30ea0.

[xci] *Ruth Etiesit Samuel, The Little Black Girls We Adored On Relaxer Boxes Are Going Viral On Twitter*, www.huffpost.com, (Oct.4, 2022), https://www.huffpost.com/entry/black-girls-relaxer-boxes-going-viral_n_633c8ee2e4b03e8038c30ea0; *Michel Martin, It turns out the models for many relaxer brands in the '90s didn't use those products*, www.npr.org, (Oct. 15, 2022), https://www.npr.org/2022/10/16/1129368784/it-turns-out-the-models-for-many-relaxer-brands-in-the-90s-didnt-use-those-produ.

[xcii] *Michel Martin, It turns out the models for many relaxer brands in the '90s didn't use those products*, www.npr.org, (Oct. 15, 2022), https://www.npr.org/2022/10/16/1129368784/it-turns-out-the-models-for-many-relaxer-brands-in-the-90s-didnt-use-those-produ.

[xciii] *Michel Martin, It turns out the models for many relaxer brands in the '90s didn't use those products*, www.npr.org, (Oct. 15, 2022), https://www.npr.org/2022/10/16/1129368784/it-turns-out-the-models-for-many-relaxer-brands-in-the-90s-didnt-use-those-produ; Strawberricurls, https://www.instagram.com/reel/CjTc-n_PXI2/?igshid=YmMyMTA2M2Y=, (Oct. 4, 2022); Attorneyawilliams, https://www.tiktok.com/t/ZTRudgrL1/ (Oct. 4, 2022).

[xciv] BETNetworks, *From $40K on wigs to $20K on Natural Hair Products, Women Explore Cost Of Black Hair Care*, (Oct. 2, 2019), youtube.com, https://www.youtube.com/watch?v=zA-zstVmRsk.

[xcv] BETNetworks, *From $40K on wigs to $20K on Natural Hair Products, Women Explore Cost Of Black Hair Care*, (Oct. 2, 2019), youtube.com, https://www.youtube.com/watch?v=zA-zstVmRsk.

[xcvi] *See Wedaeli Chibelushi, Who Dominates The World's Black Hair Industry?*, pridemagazine.com, (Aug. 10, 2018), https://www.pridemagazine.com/who-dominates-the-worlds-black-hair-industry/; Los Angeles Times, *Money flowing into the natural hair industry is a blessing and curse for those who built it up*, www.latimes.com, (Aug. 10, 2017), https://www.latimes.com/business/la-fi-natural-hair-industry-20170809-htmlstory.html; *Emma Sapong, Roots of tension: race, hair, competition and black beauty stores*, mprnews.com, (April 25, 2017 9:00 am), https://www.mprnews.org/story/2017/04/25/black-beauty-shops-korean-suppliers-roots-of-tension-mn; *See Seren Morris, From Shea Moisture to Carol's Daughter, This List of Non-Black-Owned Hair Brands May Surprise You*, www.newsweek.com, (June 20, 2020), https://www.newsweek.com/list-non-black-hair-brands-shea-moisture-carols-

daughter-1509677; *see* Karen Grigsby Bates, *A Black Cosmetic Company Sells, Or Sells Out?*, npr.org, (Oct. 24, 2014), https://www.npr.org/sections/codeswitch/2014/10/24/358263731/a-black-cosmetic-company-sells-or-sells-out.

[xcvii] *See* Karen Grigsby Bates, *A Black Cosmetic Company Sells, Or Sells Out?*, npr.org, (Oct. 24, 2014), https://www.npr.org/sections/codeswitch/2014/10/24/358263731/a-black-cosmetic-company-sells-or-sells-out;

see Seren Morris, *From Shea Moisture to Carol's Daughter, This List of Non-Black-Owned Hair Brands May Surprise You*, www.newsweek.com, (June 20, 2020), https://www.newsweek.com/list-non-black-hair-brands-shea-moisture-carols-daughter-1509677.

[xcviii] Stacy M. Brown, *Ben Crump Files Lawsuit on Behalf of Users of Chemical Hair-Straightening Products*, www.washingtoninformer.com, (Oct. 24, 2022), https://www.washingtoninformer.com/ben-crump-files-lawsuit-on-behalf-of-users-of-chemical-hair-straightening-products/.

[xcix] EWG's Skin Deep, *Think All Your Personal Care Products Are Safe? Think Again*, www.ewg.org, https://www.ewg.org/skindeep/ (last visited Apr. 26, 2022). The website allows you to search by product, brand, or chemical to get the toxicity levels of products that the organization has reviewed. *Id.*

[c] EWG's Skin Deep, *Think All Your Personal Care Products Are Safe? Think Again*, www.ewg.org, https://www.ewg.org/skindeep/ (last visited Apr. 26, 2022). The website allows you to search by product, brand, or chemical to get the toxicity levels of products that the organization has reviewed. *Id.*

[ci] Leila Fadel, *DevaCurl Faces Class Action Lawsuit Alleging Hair Loss*, www.npr.org, (Feb. 15, 2020), https://www.npr.org/2020/02/15/806366035/devacurl-faces-class-action-lawsuit-alleging-hair-loss; The curly hair movement gained traction with a product called DevaCurl that made it easy for curly hair girls to wear their natural hair. *Id.* Unfortunately, DevaCurl products turned into a scandal when its users reported hair damage and hair loss after using the product. *Id.*

[cii] Nicquel Terry Ellis, *You'll have to learn how to do textured hair to get a stylist's license in Louisiana*, (Nov. 13, 2021, updated 6:00 AM), amp.cnn.com, https://amp.cnn.com/cnn/2021/11/13/us/louisiana-textured-hair-exam/index.html.

[ciii] *See generally* Becky Freeth, *Black actresses are sharing their experiences of hairstyling in Hollywood and it's actually shocking*, (Jan. 28, 2021), Glamourmagazine.co.uk, https://www.glamourmagazine.co.uk/article/black-hair-in-hollywood; *see also* Sharareh Drury and Lindsay Weinberg, *Hollywood's Black Hair Problem on Set: "We've All Cried in Our Trailers"*, hollywoodreporter.com, (Feb. 7, 2020), https://www.hollywoodreporter.com/movies/movie-news/hollywood-s-black-hair-problem-set-we-ve-all-cried-trailers-1274876/.

[civ] *See generally* Becky Freeth, *Black actresses are sharing their experiences of*

hairstyling in Hollywood and it's actually shocking, (Jan. 28, 2021), Glamourmagazine.co.uk, https://www.glamourmagazine.co.uk/article/black-hair-in-hollywood; *see also Sharareh Drury and Lindsay Weinberg, Hollywood's Black Hair Problem on Set: "We've All Cried in Our Trailers"*, hollywoodreporter.com, (Feb. 7, 2020), https://www.hollywoodreporter.com/movies/movie-news/hollywood-s-black-hair-problem-set-we-ve-all-cried-trailers-1274876/.

[cv] *See* Not So Pretty (HBO Max 2022); *see Leila Fadel, DevaCurl Faces Class Action Lawsuit Alleging Hair Loss*, www.npr.org, (Feb. 15, 2020), https://www.npr.org/2020/02/15/806366035/devacurl-faces-class-action-lawsuit-alleging-hair-loss; There has been a push to pass the Safe Cosmetics Safety And Enhancement Act of 2019 which would ban more harmful chemicals in everyday cosmetic and personal care items and make manufacturers adhere to certain standards in the industry. H.R. 5279, 116th Congress (2020).

[cvi] *Lori Weisberg and Mike Freeman, Black job applicant in San Diego sues company for discrimination over hairstyle*, sandiegouniontribune.com, (Nov. 30, 2021, updated Dec. 1, 2021, 11:55 AM), https://www.sandiegouniontribune.com/business/story/2021-11-30/black-job-applicant-in-san-diego-sues-company-for-hair-discrimination?fbclid=IwAR3HB1QoQ3TKUQ5EA4ZhYvMEB8OhIsEOur9M1SR7XLzCvHYAYwfV7LuCp2c.

[cvii] Jeffrey A. Thornton v. Encore Group (USA), LLC, Superior Court of the State of California for the County of San Diego, Civil Case No. 37-2021-00049996-CU-OE-CTL, 11/29/2021; Thornton v. Encore Global, scribd.com, https://www.scribd.com/document/544406385/Thornton-v-Encore-Global (last visited Dec. 23, 2021).

[cviii] Jeffrey A. Thornton v. Encore Group (USA), LLC, Superior Court of the State of California for the County of San Diego, Civil Case No. 37-2021-00049996-CU-OE-CTL, 11/29/2021; Thornton v. Encore Global, scribd.com, https://www.scribd.com/document/544406385/Thornton-v-Encore-Global (last visited Dec. 23, 2021).

[cix] Jeffrey A. Thornton v. Encore Group (USA), LLC, Superior Court of the State of California for the County of San Diego, Civil Case No. 37-2021-00049996-CU-OE-CTL, 11/29/2021; Thornton v. Encore Global, scribd.com, https://www.scribd.com/document/544406385/Thornton-v-Encore-Global (last visited Dec. 23, 2021).

[cx] Jeffrey A. Thornton v. Encore Group (USA), LLC, Superior Court of the State of California for the County of San Diego, Civil Case No. 37-2021-00049996-CU-OE-CTL, 11/29/2021; Thornton v. Encore Global, scribd.com, https://www.scribd.com/document/544406385/Thornton-v-Encore-Global (last visited Dec. 23, 2021).

[cxi] Jeffrey A. Thornton v. Encore Group (USA), LLC, Superior

[cxi] Court of the State of California for the County of San Diego, Civil Case No. 37-2021-00049996-CU-OE-CTL, 11/29/2021; Thornton v. Encore Global, scribd.com, https://www.scribd.com/document/544406385/Thornton-v-Encore-Global (last visited Dec. 23, 2021).

[cxii] Jeffrey A. Thornton v. Encore Group (USA), LLC, Superior Court of the State of California for the County of San Diego, Civil Case No. 37-2021-00049996-CU-OE-CTL, 11/29/2021; Thornton v. Encore Global, scribd.com, https://www.scribd.com/document/544406385/Thornton-v-Encore-Global (last visited Dec. 23, 2021).

[cxiii] Jeffrey A. Thornton v. Encore Group (USA), LLC, Superior Court of the State of California for the County of San Diego, Civil Case No. 37-2021-00049996-CU-OE-CTL, 11/29/2021; Thornton v. Encore Global, scribd.com, https://www.scribd.com/document/544406385/Thornton-v-Encore-Global (last visited Dec. 23, 2021).

[cxiv] Jeffrey A. Thornton v. Encore Group (USA), LLC, Superior Court of the State of California for the County of San Diego, Civil Case No. 37-2021-00049996-CU-OE-CTL, 11/29/2021; Thornton v. Encore Global, scribd.com, https://www.scribd.com/document/544406385/Thornton-v-Encore-Global (last visited Dec. 23, 2021).

[cxv] Jeffrey A. Thornton v. Encore Group (USA), LLC, Superior Court of the State of California for the County of San Diego, Civil Case No. 37-2021-00049996-CU-OE-CTL, 11/29/2021; Thornton v. Encore Global, scribd.com, https://www.scribd.com/document/544406385/Thornton-v-Encore-Global (last visited Dec. 23, 2021).

[cxvi] Kristopher J. Brooks, *San Diego man sues employer for discrimination over natural hair style*, www.cbsnews.com, (Dec. 6, 2021), https://www.cbsnews.com/news/jeffrey-thornton-lawsuit-crown-act-encore-global/.

[cxvii] Kristopher J. Brooks, *San Diego man sues employer for discrimination over natural hair style*, www.cbsnews.com, (Dec. 6, 2021), https://www.cbsnews.com/news/jeffrey-thornton-lawsuit-crown-act-encore-global/.

[cxviii] *See generally* Dawn Ennis, *United Airlines Gives All Flight Attendants OK For Tattoos, Nail Polish And Makeup*, forbes.com, (Aug. 10, 2021, 9:45 PM), https://www.forbes.com/sites/dawnstaceyennis/2021/08/10/united-airlines-gives-all-flight-attendants-ok-for-tattoos-nail-polish-and-makeup/amp/.

[cxix] *See* Rogers v. American Airlines, Inc., 527 F. Supp. 229 (SDNY 1981).

[cxx] *See* Rogers v. American Airlines, Inc., 527 F. Supp. 229 (SDNY 1981).

[cxxi] Dawn Ennis, *United Airlines Gives All Flight Attendants OK For Tattoos, Nail Polish And Makeup*, forbes.com, (Aug. 10, 2021, 9:45 PM), https://www.forbes.com/sites/dawnstaceyennis/2021/08/10/united-airlines-gives-all-flight-attendants-ok-for-tattoos-nail-polish-and-makeup/amp/.

[cxxii] Dawn Ennis, *United Airlines Gives All Flight Attendants OK For Tattoos, Nail Polish And Makeup*, forbes.com, (Aug. 10, 2021, 9:45 PM), https://www.forbes.com/sites/dawnstaceyennis/2021/08/10/united-airlines-

gives-all-flight-attendants-ok-for-tattoos-nail-polish-and-makeup/amp/.

[cxxiii] *Sanestine Hunter and Jacque Porter, Federal agency sues Louisiana company over hair discrimination,* https://www.arklatexhomepage.com/news/local-news/federal-agency-sues-louisiana-company-over-hair-discrimination/amp/ (last visited Dec. 26, 2021).

[cxxiv] *Sanestine Hunter and Jacque Porter, Federal agency sues Louisiana company over hair discrimination,* https://www.arklatexhomepage.com/news/local-news/federal-agency-sues-louisiana-company-over-hair-discrimination/amp/ (last visited Dec. 26, 2021).

[cxxv] *Sanestine Hunter and Jacque Porter, Federal agency sues Louisiana company over hair discrimination,* https://www.arklatexhomepage.com/news/local-news/federal-agency-sues-louisiana-company-over-hair-discrimination/amp/ (last visited Dec. 26, 2021).

[cxxvi] *Sanestine Hunter and Jacque Porter, Federal agency sues Louisiana company over hair discrimination,* https://www.arklatexhomepage.com/news/local-news/federal-agency-sues-louisiana-company-over-hair-discrimination/amp/ (last visited Dec. 26, 2021).

[cxxvii] *Andre P. Burnside, CROWN Act Ordinance: New Orleans Enacts Law to Prohibit Hairstyle Discrimination,* ogletree.com, (Jan. 15, 2021), https://ogletree.com/insights/crown-act-ordinance-new-orleans-enacts-law-to-prohibit-hairstyle-discrimination/; *About, CROWN Coalition,* https://www.thecrownact.com/about (last visited July. 23, 2022); *Virginia Langmaid, Massachusetts becomes latest state to ban discrimination based on natural hairstyles,* www.cnn.com, (July 26, 2022),

[cxxviii] *Krista Frost, Prominent Columbus women share stories of hair discrimination,* www.10tv.com, (Nov. 19, 2021), https://www.10tv.com/amp/article/news/local/prominent-columbus-women-share-stories-hair-discrimination/530-620bf6b8-f159-4300-8678-b586f56d8b41.

[cxxix] Roundtable Discussion: Prominent Columbus women share stories of hair discrimination, WBNS 10TV, (Nov. 2021), Youtube.com, https://www.youtube.com/watch?v=qS_z8OOzZ6w.

[cxxx] Roundtable Discussion: Prominent Columbus women share stories of hair discrimination, WBNS 10TV, (Nov. 2021), Youtube.com, https://www.youtube.com/watch?v=qS_z8OOzZ6w.

[cxxxi] Roundtable Discussion: Prominent Columbus women share stories of hair discrimination, WBNS 10TV, (Nov. 2021), Youtube.com, https://www.youtube.com/watch?v=qS_z8OOzZ6w.

[cxxxii] *Office Of Academic Affairs, The CROWN Act and Ohio State's expectations,* oaa.osu.edu, (March 10, 2021), https://oaa.osu.edu/crown-act-and-ohio-states-expectations;

[cxxxiii] *Tashara Parker, Rooted: Judge Amber Givens was told 'your hair is going to offend voters,' she explains in her hair story,* wfaa.com, (Feb. 25, 2021), https://www.wfaa.com/article/news/community/rooted/rooted-judge-amber-givens-

was-told-your-hair-is-going-to-offend-voters-she-explains-in-her-hair-story/287-f2f11584-d012-4e86-9cdc-048e0619db60.

[cxxxiv] *Tashara Parker, Rooted: Judge Amber Givens was told 'your hair is going to offend voters,' she explains in her hair story*, wfaa.com, (Feb. 25, 2021), https://www.wfaa.com/article/news/community/rooted/rooted-judge-amber-givens-was-told-your-hair-is-going-to-offend-voters-she-explains-in-her-hair-story/287-f2f11584-d012-4e86-9cdc-048e0619db60.

[cxxxv] *Tashara Parker, Rooted: Police officer never thought his braided hair would interfere with his ability to do his job*, www.wfaa.com, (May 6, 2021), https://www.wfaa.com/article/news/community/rooted/rooted-dart-police-officer-dakari-davis-shares-his-hair-story/287-95c60988-f7df-4a40-9db3-e9ed7f14101c.

[cxxxvi] *Tashara Parker, Rooted: Police officer never thought his braided hair would interfere with his ability to do his job*, www.wfaa.com, (May 6, 2021), https://www.wfaa.com/article/news/community/rooted/rooted-dart-police-officer-dakari-davis-shares-his-hair-story/287-95c60988-f7df-4a40-9db3-e9ed7f14101c.

[cxxxvii] *Tashara Parker, Rooted: Police officer never thought his braided hair would interfere with his ability to do his job*, www.wfaa.com, (May 6, 2021), https://www.wfaa.com/article/news/community/rooted/rooted-dart-police-officer-dakari-davis-shares-his-hair-story/287-95c60988-f7df-4a40-9db3-e9ed7f14101c.

[cxxxviii] *Tashara Parker, Rooted: Police officer never thought his braided hair would interfere with his ability to do his job*, www.wfaa.com, (May 6, 2021), https://www.wfaa.com/article/news/community/rooted/rooted-dart-police-officer-dakari-davis-shares-his-hair-story/287-95c60988-f7df-4a40-9db3-e9ed7f14101c.

[cxxxix] *Tashara Parker, Rooted: Police officer never thought his braided hair would interfere with his ability to do his job*, www.wfaa.com, (May 6, 2021), https://www.wfaa.com/article/news/community/rooted/rooted-dart-police-officer-dakari-davis-shares-his-hair-story/287-95c60988-f7df-4a40-9db3-e9ed7f14101c.

[cxl] *Tashara Parker, Rooted: Police officer never thought his braided hair would interfere with his ability to do his job*, www.wfaa.com, (May 6, 2021), https://www.wfaa.com/article/news/community/rooted/rooted-dart-police-officer-dakari-davis-shares-his-hair-story/287-95c60988-f7df-4a40-9db3-e9ed7f14101c.

[cxli] *Lorna Sheridan, MacArthur Place job seeker alleges hairstyle was questioned*, sonomannews.com, (March 26, 2021), https://www.sonomanews.com/article/news/macarthur-place-job-seeker-alleges-hairstyle-was-questioned/.

[cxlii] *Lorna Sheridan, MacArthur Place job seeker alleges hairstyle was questioned*, sonomannews.com, (March 26, 2021), https://www.sonomanews.com/article/news/macarthur-place-job-seeker-alleges-hairstyle-was-questioned/.

[cxliii] *Lorna Sheridan, MacArthur Place job seeker alleges hairstyle was questioned*, sonomannews.com, (March 26, 2021), https://www.sonomanews.com/article/news/macarthur-place-job-seeker-alleges-hairstyle-was-questioned/.

[cxliv] *Lorna Sheridan, MacArthur Place job seeker alleges hairstyle was questioned*, sonomannews.com, (March 26, 2021), https://www.sonomanews.com/article/news/macarthur-place-job-seeker-alleges-hairstyle-was-questioned/.

[cxlv] *Lorna Sheridan, MacArthur Place job seeker alleges hairstyle was questioned*, sonomannews.com, (March 26, 2021), https://www.sonomanews.com/article/news/macarthur-place-job-seeker-alleges-hairstyle-was-questioned/.

[cxlvi] *Lorna Sheridan, MacArthur Place job seeker alleges hairstyle was questioned*, sonomannews.com, (March 26, 2021), https://www.sonomanews.com/article/news/macarthur-place-job-seeker-alleges-hairstyle-was-questioned/.

[cxlvii] *Lorna Sheridan, MacArthur Place job seeker alleges hairstyle was questioned*, sonomannews.com, (March 26, 2021), https://www.sonomanews.com/article/news/macarthur-place-job-seeker-alleges-hairstyle-was-questioned/.

[cxlviii] *James Doubek, The Army Is Expanding Allowed Hairstyles For Women*, www.npr.com, (May 23, 2021), https://www.npr.org/2021/05/23/999313152/the-army-is-expanding-allowed-hairstyles-for-women.

[cxlix] *James Doubek, The Army Is Expanding Allowed Hairstyles For Women*, www.npr.com, (May 23, 2021), https://www.npr.org/2021/05/23/999313152/the-army-is-expanding-allowed-hairstyles-for-women.

[cl] *Sylvia Obell, Navy Discharges Black Sailor For Refusing to Cut Her Natural Hair*, essence.com, (Oct. 27, 2020), https://www.essence.com/news/mom-rents-billboard-to-celebrate-doctor-daughter/.

[cli] *Sylvia Obell, Navy Discharges Black Sailor For Refusing to Cut Her Natural Hair*, essence.com, (Oct. 27, 2020), https://www.essence.com/news/mom-rents-billboard-to-celebrate-doctor-daughter/.

[clii] *Sylvia Obell, Navy Discharges Black Sailor For Refusing to Cut Her Natural Hair*, essence.com, (Oct. 27, 2020), https://www.essence.com/news/mom-rents-billboard-to-celebrate-doctor-daughter/.

[cliii] *Sylvia Obell, Navy Discharges Black Sailor For Refusing to Cut Her Natural Hair*, essence.com, (Oct. 27, 2020), https://www.essence.com/news/mom-rents-billboard-to-celebrate-doctor-daughter/.

[cliv] The author acknowledges that there are certain rules and protocols that have to be followed by members of the armed forces to protect Americans.

[clv] *See Maya Allen, 22 Corporate Women Share What Wearing Their Natural Hair to Work Means*, www.byrdie.com, https://www.byrdie.com/natural-hair-in-corporate-america (Updated Dec. 4, 2021).

[clvi] Alexandra Jaffe, *Karine Jean-Pierre makes history by leading White House press briefing*, www.wfaa.com, (May 26, 2021, 3:10 PM, updated May 26, 2021, 3:27

PM), https://www.wfaa.com/article/news/nation-world/karine-jean-pierre-makes-history-white-house-briefing/507-6b389c0d-cd48-4ab9-a716-0648c6914dc0.

[clvii] Alexandra Jaffe, *Karine Jean-Pierre makes history by leading White House press briefing*, www.wfaa.com, (May 26, 2021, 3:10 PM, updated May 26, 2021, 3:27 PM), https://www.wfaa.com/article/news/nation-world/karine-jean-pierre-makes-history-white-house-briefing/507-6b389c0d-cd48-4ab9-a716-0648c6914dc0.

[clviii] *The White House, President Biden Announces Karine Jean-Pierre as White House Press Secretary*, www.whitehouse.gov, (May 5, 2022), https://www.whitehouse.gov/briefing-room/statements-releases/2022/05/05/president-biden-announces-karine-jean-pierre-as-white-house-press-secretary/.

[clix] *See Jacqueline Laurean Yates, Michelle Obama's braids have a big moment during her White House portrait unveiling*, www.goodmorningamerica.com, (Sept. 8, 2022), https://www.goodmorningamerica.com/style/story/michelle-obamas-braids-big-moment-white-house-portrait-89519020; see Angela Johnson, *If Michelle Obama Can Wear Braids to the White House, Shouldn't We Be Able to Wear Our Braids to Work?*, www.theroot.com, (Sept. 8, 2022), https://www.theroot.com/if-michelle-obama-can-wear-braids-to-the-white-houses-1849512281.

[clx] *See Jacqueline Laurean Yates, Michelle Obama's braids have a big moment during her White House portrait unveiling*, www.goodmorningamerica.com, (Sept. 8, 2022), https://www.goodmorningamerica.com/style/story/michelle-obamas-braids-big-moment-white-house-portrait-89519020; see Angela Johnson, *If Michelle Obama Can Wear Braids to the White House, Shouldn't We Be Able to Wear Our Braids to Work?*, www.theroot.com, (Sept. 8, 2022), https://www.theroot.com/if-michelle-obama-can-wear-braids-to-the-white-houses-1849512281.

[clxi] Victoria W. Wolcott (2001). *Remaking Respectability: African American Women in Interwar Detroit*. Univ of North Carolina Press. pp. 5–7. ISBN 978-0-8078-4966-8.

[clxii] *See* Janice Gassam Asare, *Our Obsession With Black Excellence Is Harming Black People*, forbes.com, (Aug 1, 2021,11:20pm), https://www.forbes.com/sites/janicegassam/2021/08/01/our-obsession-with-black-excellence-is-harming-black-people/?sh=11892e62fd99.

[clxiii] *Associated Press*, Florida city repeals 13-year ban on saggy pants; signs still warn against it, usatoday.com, Sept. 14, 2020, updated Sept 15, 2020), www.usatoday.com, https://www.usatoday.com/story/news/nation/2020/09/14/opa-locka-florida-repeals-ban-saggy-pants-but-signs-still-stand/5791448002/; *Sara MacNeil*, Sagging pants law abolished in Shreveport, (June 11, 2019 updated June 12, 2019), www.shreveporttimes.com, https://www.shreveporttimes.com/story/news/2019/06/11/sagging-pants-

law-abolished-shreveport/1425135001/.

[clxiv] *Associated Press*, Florida city repeals 13-year ban on saggy pants; signs still warn against it, usatoday.com, Sept. 14, 2020, updated Sept 15, 2020), www.usatoday.com, https://www.usatoday.com/story/news/nation/2020/09/14/opa-locka-florida-repeals-ban-saggy-pants-but-signs-still-stand/5791448002/; *Sara MacNeil*, Sagging pants law abolished in Shreveport, (June 11, 2019 updated June 12, 2019), www.shreveporttimes.com, https://www.shreveporttimes.com/story/news/2019/06/11/sagging-pants-law-abolished-shreveport/1425135001/.

[clxv] *Teryn Payne, Kim Kardashian West Responds to the Backlash Over Her Braids*, www.glamour.com, (June 21, 2018), https://www.glamour.com/story/kim-kardashian-braids-explanation.

[clxvi] *Teryn Payne, Kim Kardashian West Responds to the Backlash Over Her Braids*, www.glamour.com, (June 21, 2018), https://www.glamour.com/story/kim-kardashian-braids-explanation.

[clxvii] *See Teryn Payne, Kim Kardashian West Responds to the Backlash Over Her Braids*, www.glamour.com, (June 21, 2018), https://www.glamour.com/story/kim-kardashian-braids-explanation.

[clxviii] *Dove, The CROWN Research Study for Girls*, www.dove.com, https://www.dove.com/us/en/stories/about-dove/hair-discrimination-research.html (last visited Sept. 17, 2022).

[clxix] *See Dove, The CROWN Research Study for Girls*, www.dove.com, https://www.dove.com/us/en/stories/about-dove/hair-discrimination-research.html (last visited Sept. 17, 2022).

[clxx] *Dove, The CROWN Research Study for Girls*, www.dove.com, https://www.dove.com/us/en/stories/about-dove/hair-discrimination-research.html (last visited Sept. 17, 2022).

[clxxi] *Dove, The CROWN Research Study for Girls*, www.dove.com, https://www.dove.com/us/en/stories/about-dove/hair-discrimination-research.html (last visited Sept. 17, 2022).

[clxxii] *Tim Morris, School has the right to enforce dress code on hair extensions*, www.nola.com, (Aug. 25, 2018), https://www.nola.com/opinions/article_19556de3-5121-531b-995f-404cd9e5a6ce.html.

[clxxiii] *Tim Morris, School has the right to enforce dress code on hair extensions*, www.nola.com, (Aug. 25, 2018), https://www.nola.com/opinions/article_19556de3-5121-531b-995f-404cd9e5a6ce.html.

[clxxiv] *See* Civil Rights Act of 1964 42 U.S.C. § 2000e (1964); *see Peter Greene, SCOTUS Gives Private Religious Schools The Okay To Discriminate Freely*, forbes.com, (July 16, 2020), https://www.forbes.com/sites/petergreene/2020/07/16/scotus-gives-private-religious-schools-the-okay-to-discriminate-freely/; *Tim Morris, School has the right to enforce dress code on hair extensions*, www.nola.com, (Aug. 25, 2018), https://www.nola.com/opinions/article_19556de3-5121-531b-995f-404cd9e5a6ce.html.

[clxxv] See Tim Morris, *School has the right to enforce dress code on hair extensions,* www.nola.com, (Aug. 25, 2018), https://www.nola.com/opinions/article_19556de3-5121-531b-995f-404cd9e5a6ce.html.

[clxxvi] *Tim Morris, School has the right to enforce dress code on hair extensions,* www.nola.com, (Aug. 25, 2018), https://www.nola.com/opinions/article_19556de3-5121-531b-995f-404cd9e5a6ce.html.

[clxxvii] *See generally Tim Morris, School has the right to enforce dress code on hair extensions,* www.nola.com, (Aug. 25, 2018), https://www.nola.com/opinions/article_19556de3-5121-531b-995f-404cd9e5a6ce.html.

[clxxviii] Taliah Waajid, *Protective Styling: Why You Should Wear Protective Styles,* naturalhair.org, (July 21, 2020), https://naturalhair.org/blogs/news/protective-stylng-why-you-should-wear-protective-styles.

[clxxix] *Eric Ortiz, N.J. wrestler forced to cut dreadlocks still targeted over hair, lawyer says,* www.nbcnews.com, (Jan. 10, 2019), https://www.nbcnews.com/news/nbcblk/n-j-wrestler-forced-cut-dreadlocks-still-targeted-over-hair-n957116.

[clxxx] *Eric Ortiz, N.J. wrestler forced to cut dreadlocks still targeted over hair, lawyer says,* www.nbcnews.com, (Jan. 10, 2019), https://www.nbcnews.com/news/nbcblk/n-j-wrestler-forced-cut-dreadlocks-still-targeted-over-hair-n957116.

[clxxxi] *Eric Ortiz, N.J. wrestler forced to cut dreadlocks still targeted over hair, lawyer says,* www.nbcnews.com, (Jan. 10, 2019), https://www.nbcnews.com/news/nbcblk/n-j-wrestler-forced-cut-dreadlocks-still-targeted-over-hair-n957116.

[clxxxii] *Eric Ortiz, N.J. wrestler forced to cut dreadlocks still targeted over hair, lawyer says,* www.nbcnews.com, (Jan. 10, 2019), https://www.nbcnews.com/news/nbcblk/n-j-wrestler-forced-cut-dreadlocks-still-targeted-over-hair-n957116.

[clxxxiii] Eric Ortiz, N.J. wrestler forced to cut dreadlocks still targeted over hair, lawyer says, www.nbcnews.com, (Jan. 10, 2019), https://www.nbcnews.com/news/nbcblk/n-j-wrestler-forced-cut-dreadlocks-still-targeted-over-hair-n957116.

[clxxxiv] Eric Ortiz, N.J. wrestler forced to cut dreadlocks still targeted over hair, lawyer says, www.nbcnews.com, (Jan. 10, 2019), https://www.nbcnews.com/news/nbcblk/n-j-wrestler-forced-cut-dreadlocks-still-targeted-over-hair-n957116.

[clxxxv] *Eric Ortiz, N.J. wrestler forced to cut dreadlocks still targeted over hair, lawyer says,* www.nbcnews.com, (Jan. 10, 2019), https://www.nbcnews.com/news/nbcblk/n-j-wrestler-forced-cut-dreadlocks-still-targeted-over-hair-n957116.

[clxxxvi] Eric Ortiz, N.J. wrestler forced to cut dreadlocks still targeted over hair, lawyer says, www.nbcnews.com, (Jan. 10, 2019), https://www.nbcnews.com/news/nbcblk/n-j-wrestler-forced-cut-dreadlocks-still-targeted-over-hair-n957116.

[clxxxvii] *Chrissy Callahan, Tiffany L. Brown fights Texas elementary school's policy to cut son's dreadlocks,* www.today.com, (Jan. 16, 2019), https://www.today.com/style/tiffany-l-brown-fights-texas-elementary-school-s-policy-cut-t146837.

[clxxxviii] *Chrissy Callahan, Tiffany L. Brown fights Texas elementary school's policy to cut son's dreadlocks, www.today.com, (Jan. 16, 2019), https://www.today.com/style/tiffany-l-brown-fights-texas-elementary-school-s-policy-cut-t146837.*

[clxxxix] *Chrissy Callahan, Tiffany L. Brown fights Texas elementary school's policy to cut son's dreadlocks, www.today.com, (Jan. 16, 2019), https://www.today.com/style/tiffany-l-brown-fights-texas-elementary-school-s-policy-cut-t146837.*

[cxc] *Chrissy Callahan, Tiffany L. Brown fights Texas elementary school's policy to cut son's dreadlocks, www.today.com, (Jan. 16, 2019), https://www.today.com/style/tiffany-l-brown-fights-texas-elementary-school-s-policy-cut-t146837.*

[cxci] *Chrissy Callahan, Tiffany L. Brown fights Texas elementary school's policy to cut son's dreadlocks, www.today.com, (Jan. 16, 2019), https://www.today.com/style/tiffany-l-brown-fights-texas-elementary-school-s-policy-cut-t146837.*

[cxcii] *Chrissy Callahan, Tiffany L. Brown fights Texas elementary school's policy to cut son's dreadlocks, www.today.com, (Jan. 16, 2019), https://www.today.com/style/tiffany-l-brown-fights-texas-elementary-school-s-policy-cut-t146837.*

[cxciii] *Chrissy Callahan, Tiffany L. Brown fights Texas elementary school's policy to cut son's dreadlocks, www.today.com, (Jan. 16, 2019), https://www.today.com/style/tiffany-l-brown-fights-texas-elementary-school-s-policy-cut-t146837.*

[cxciv] *Chrissy Callahan, Tiffany L. Brown fights Texas elementary school's policy to cut son's dreadlocks, www.today.com, (Jan. 16, 2019), https://www.today.com/style/tiffany-l-brown-fights-texas-elementary-school-s-policy-cut-t146837.*

[cxcv] *Chrissy Callahan, Tiffany L. Brown fights Texas elementary school's policy to cut son's dreadlocks, www.today.com, (Jan. 16, 2019), https://www.today.com/style/tiffany-l-brown-fights-texas-elementary-school-s-policy-cut-t146837.*

[cxcvi] *Chrissy Callahan, Tiffany L. Brown fights Texas elementary school's policy to cut son's dreadlocks, www.today.com, (Jan. 16, 2019), https://www.today.com/style/tiffany-l-brown-fights-texas-elementary-school-s-policy-cut-t146837.*

[cxcvii] *Chrissy Callahan, Tiffany L. Brown fights Texas elementary school's policy to cut son's dreadlocks, www.today.com, (Jan. 16, 2019), https://www.today.com/style/tiffany-l-brown-fights-texas-elementary-school-s-policy-cut-t146837.*

[cxcviii] *Chrissy Callahan, Tiffany L. Brown fights Texas elementary school's policy to cut son's dreadlocks, www.today.com, (Jan. 16, 2019), https://www.today.com/style/tiffany-l-brown-fights-texas-elementary-school-s-policy-cut-t146837.*

[cxcix] *Chrissy Callahan, Tiffany L. Brown fights Texas elementary school's policy to cut son's dreadlocks, www.today.com, (Jan. 16, 2019), https://www.today.com/style/tiffany-l-brown-fights-texas-elementary-school-s-policy-cut-t146837.*

[cc] *Chrissy Callahan, Tiffany L. Brown fights Texas elementary school's policy to cut son's dreadlocks, www.today.com, (Jan. 16, 2019), https://www.today.com/style/tiffany-l-brown-fights-texas-elementary-school-s-policy-cut-t146837.*

[cci] *Chrissy Callahan, Tiffany L. Brown fights Texas elementary school's policy to cut son's dreadlocks, www.today.com, (Jan. 16, 2019), https://www.today.com/*

style/tiffany-l-brown-fights-texas-elementary-school-s-policy-cut-t146837.

[ccii] *See U.S. Dept. of Edu., Title IX and Sex Discrimination*, (Revised August 2021), https://www2.ed.gov/about/offices/list/ocr/docs/tix_dis.html; Chrissy Callahan, *Tiffany L. Brown fights Texas elementary school's policy to cut son's dreadlocks*, www.today.com, (Jan. 16, 2019), https://www.today.com/style/tiffany-l-brown-fights-texas-elementary-school-s-policy-cut-t146837.

[cciii] Chrissy Callahan, *Tiffany L. Brown fights Texas elementary school's policy to cut son's dreadlocks*, www.today.com, (Jan. 16, 2019), https://www.today.com/style/tiffany-l-brown-fights-texas-elementary-school-s-policy-cut-t146837.

[cciv] *Tiffany Brown, Stop gender discrimination and liberate male hair in the Midway ISD Dress Code policy*, www.change.org, https://www.change.org/p/stop-gender-discrimination-and-liberate-male-hair-in-the-midway-isd-dress-code-policy (last visited Mar. 25, 2022).

[ccv] Matthew S. Schwartz, *Texas School Board Keeps Grooming Code That Led To Suspension Of Black Students*, www.npr.org, (July 22, 2020), https://www.npr.org/2020/07/22/893970329/texas-school-board-keeps-grooming-code-that-led-to-suspension-of-black-students.

[ccvi] Matthew S. Schwartz, *Texas School Board Keeps Grooming Code That Led To Suspension Of Black Students*, www.npr.org, (July 22, 2020), https://www.npr.org/2020/07/22/893970329/texas-school-board-keeps-grooming-code-that-led-to-suspension-of-black-students.

[ccvii] Matthew S. Schwartz, *Texas School Board Keeps Grooming Code That Led To Suspension Of Black Students*, www.npr.org, (July 22, 2020), https://www.npr.org/2020/07/22/893970329/texas-school-board-keeps-grooming-code-that-led-to-suspension-of-black-students.

[ccviii] Matthew S. Schwartz, *Texas School Board Keeps Grooming Code That Led To Suspension Of Black Students*, www.npr.org, (July 22, 2020), https://www.npr.org/2020/07/22/893970329/texas-school-board-keeps-grooming-code-that-led-to-suspension-of-black-students.

[ccix] Jamie E. Galvan, *Court rules Barbers Hill High School student does not have to cut his locs*, www.khou.com, (Aug. 18, 2020), https://www.khou.com/article/news/local/court-rules-barbers-hill-high-school-student-does-not-have-to-cut-his-locs/285-b4c29c9b-9c98-4236-a2cf-05802cf1cbb0; Matthew S. Schwartz, *Texas School Board Keeps Grooming Code That Led To Suspension Of Black Students*, www.npr.org, (July 22, 2020), https://www.npr.org/2020/07/22/893970329/texas-school-board-keeps-grooming-code-that-led-to-suspension-of-black-students.

[ccx] Jamie E. Galvan, *Court rules Barbers Hill High School student does not have to cut his locs*, www.khou.com, (Aug. 18, 2020), https://www.khou.com/article/news/local/court-rules-barbers-hill-high-school-student-does-not-have-to-cut-his-locs/285-b4c29c9b-9c98-4236-a2cf-05802cf1cbb0; Matthew S. Schwartz, *Texas School Board Keeps Grooming Code That Led To Suspension Of Black*

[ccxi] *Jamie E. Galvan, Court rules Barbers Hill High School student does not have to cut his locs*, www.khou.com, (Aug. 18, 2020), https://www.khou.com/article/news/local/court-rules-barbers-hill-high-school-student-does-not-have-to-cut-his-locs/285-b4c29c9b-9c98-4236-a2cf-05802cf1cbb0; Matthew S. Schwartz, *Texas School Board Keeps Grooming Code That Led To Suspension Of Black Students*, www.npr.org, (July 22, 2020), https://www.npr.org/2020/07/22/893970329/texas-school-board-keeps-grooming-code-that-led-to-suspension-of-black-students.

[ccxii] *Jamie E. Galvan, Court rules Barbers Hill High School student does not have to cut his locs*, www.khou.com, (Aug. 18, 2020), https://www.khou.com/article/news/local/court-rules-barbers-hill-high-school-student-does-not-have-to-cut-his-locs/285-b4c29c9b-9c98-4236-a2cf-05802cf1cbb0; Matthew S. Schwartz, *Texas School Board Keeps Grooming Code That Led To Suspension Of Black Students*, www.npr.org, (July 22, 2020), https://www.npr.org/2020/07/22/893970329/texas-school-board-keeps-grooming-code-that-led-to-suspension-of-black-students; *Wendy Greene, Director of the center for law, policy and social action: Law Professor*, www.Drexel.edu, https://drexel.edu/law/faculty/fulltime_fac/wendy-greene/ (last visited Sept. 20, 2022).

[ccxiii] *Jamie E. Galvan, Court rules Barbers Hill High School student does not have to cut his locs*, www.khou.com, (Aug. 18, 2020), https://www.khou.com/article/news/local/court-rules-barbers-hill-high-school-student-does-not-have-to-cut-his-locs/285-b4c29c9b-9c98-4236-a2cf-05802cf1cbb0; Matthew S. Schwartz, *Texas School Board Keeps Grooming Code That Led To Suspension Of Black Students*, www.npr.org, (July 22, 2020), https://www.npr.org/2020/07/22/893970329/texas-school-board-keeps-grooming-code-that-led-to-suspension-of-black-students.

[ccxiv] *Jamie E. Galvan, Court rules Barbers Hill High School student does not have to cut his locs*, www.khou.com, (Aug. 18, 2020), https://www.khou.com/article/news/local/court-rules-barbers-hill-high-school-student-does-not-have-to-cut-his-locs/285-b4c29c9b-9c98-4236-a2cf-05802cf1cbb0; Matthew S. Schwartz, *Texas School Board Keeps Grooming Code That Led To Suspension Of Black Students*, www.npr.org, (July 22, 2020), https://www.npr.org/2020/07/22/893970329/texas-school-board-keeps-grooming-code-that-led-to-suspension-of-black-students.

[ccxv] *Tashara Parker, Rooted: Troy mother seeks changes to dress-code policy after son is placed in-school suspension over hairstyle*, www.wfaa.com, (April 21, 2021), https://www.wfaa.com/article/news/community/rooted/rooted-troy-isd-hair-style-policy-crown-act-hope-cozart/287-4d30548f-7543-402a-a6e0-eda6922d239e; *Jarell Baker, 11-year-old allowed back in class after almost two week suspension for braided hairstyle*, www.kxxv.com, (last updated April 23,

2021), https://www.kxxv.com/hometown/bell-county/11-year-old-allowed-back-in-class-after-almost-two-week-suspension-for-braided-hairstyle.

[ccxvi] *Tashara Parker, Rooted: Troy mother seeks changes to dress-code policy after son is placed in-school suspension over hairstyle*, www.wfaa.com, (April 21, 2021), https://www.wfaa.com/article/news/community/rooted/rooted-troy-isd-hair-style-policy-crown-act-hope-cozart/287-4d30548f-7543-402a-a6e0-eda6922d239e; *Jarell Baker, 11-year-old allowed back in class after almost two week suspension for braided hairstyle*, www.kxxv.com, (last updated April 23, 2021), https://www.kxxv.com/hometown/bell-county/11-year-old-allowed-back-in-class-after-almost-two-week-suspension-for-braided-hairstyle.

[ccxvii] *Tashara Parker, Rooted: Troy mother seeks changes to dress-code policy after son is placed in-school suspension over hairstyle*, www.wfaa.com, (April 21, 2021), https://www.wfaa.com/article/news/community/rooted/rooted-troy-isd-hair-style-policy-crown-act-hope-cozart/287-4d30548f-7543-402a-a6e0-eda6922d239e; *Jarell Baker, 11-year-old allowed back in class after almost two week suspension for braided hairstyle*, www.kxxv.com, (last updated April 23, 2021), https://www.kxxv.com/hometown/bell-county/11-year-old-allowed-back-in-class-after-almost-two-week-suspension-for-braided-hairstyle.

[ccxviii] *Tashara Parker, Rooted: Troy mother seeks changes to dress-code policy after son is placed in-school suspension over hairstyle*, www.wfaa.com, (April 21, 2021), https://www.wfaa.com/article/news/community/rooted/rooted-troy-isd-hair-style-policy-crown-act-hope-cozart/287-4d30548f-7543-402a-a6e0-eda6922d239e; *Jarell Baker, 11-year-old allowed back in class after almost two week suspension for braided hairstyle*, www.kxxv.com, (last updated April 23, 2021), https://www.kxxv.com/hometown/bell-county/11-year-old-allowed-back-in-class-after-almost-two-week-suspension-for-braided-hairstyle.

[ccxix] *Alisha Ebrahimji, Texas high school policy banning braided or twisted hair has stopped a teen from attending school, his mom says*, www.cnn.com, (April 29, 2022), https://amp.cnn.com/cnn/2022/04/28/us/texas-high-school-east-bernard-braided-hair-ban/index.html.

[ccxx] *Alisha Ebrahimji, Texas high school policy banning braided or twisted hair has stopped a teen from attending school, his mom says*, www.cnn.com, (April 29, 2022), https://amp.cnn.com/cnn/2022/04/28/us/texas-high-school-east-bernard-braided-hair-ban/index.html.

[ccxxi] *Alisha Ebrahimji, Texas high school policy banning braided or twisted hair has stopped a teen from attending school, his mom says*, www.cnn.com, (April 29, 2022), https://amp.cnn.com/cnn/2022/04/28/us/texas-high-school-east-bernard-braided-hair-ban/index.html.

[ccxxii] *Alisha Ebrahimji, Texas high school policy banning braided or twisted hair has stopped a teen from attending school, his mom says*, www.cnn.com, (April 29, 2022), https://amp.cnn.com/cnn/2022/04/28/us/texas-high-school-east-bernard-braided-hair-ban/index.html.

[ccxxiii] *Alisha Ebrahimji, Texas high school policy banning braided or twisted hair*

[ccxxiii continued] has stopped a teen from attending school, his mom says, www.cnn.com, (April 29, 2022), https://amp.cnn.com/cnn/2022/04/28/us/texas-high-school-east-bernard-braided-hair-ban/index.html.

[ccxxiv] *Alisha Ebrahimji, Texas high school policy banning braided or twisted hair has stopped a teen from attending school, his mom says*, www.cnn.com, (April 29, 2022), https://amp.cnn.com/cnn/2022/04/28/us/texas-high-school-east-bernard-braided-hair-ban/index.html.

[ccxxv] *Alisha Ebrahimji, Texas high school policy banning braided or twisted hair has stopped a teen from attending school, his mom says*, www.cnn.com, (April 29, 2022), https://amp.cnn.com/cnn/2022/04/28/us/texas-high-school-east-bernard-braided-hair-ban/index.html.

[ccxxvi] *The Grio Staff, School policy banning locs removed from website after teen's mom goes public*, thegrio.com, (May 5, 2022), https://thegrio.com/2022/05/05/school-policy-banning-locs-removed-from-website/?utm_source=facebook&utm_medium=news_tab.

[ccxxvii] *Taylor Ardrey, A Black Texas teen was suspended from school and told he couldn't attend graduation due to the length of his hair*, businessinsider.in, (May 11, 2022), https://www.businessinsider.in/international/news/a-black-texas-teen-was-suspended-from-school-and-told-he-couldnt-attend-graduation-due-to-the-length-of-his-hair/articleshow/91497948.cms.

[ccxxviii] *Taylor Ardrey, A Black Texas teen was suspended from school and told he couldn't attend graduation due to the length of his hair*, businessinsider.in, (May 11, 2022), https://www.businessinsider.in/international/news/a-black-texas-teen-was-suspended-from-school-and-told-he-couldnt-attend-graduation-due-to-the-length-of-his-hair/articleshow/91497948.cms.

[ccxxix] *Taylor Ardrey, A Black Texas teen was suspended from school and told he couldn't attend graduation due to the length of his hair*, businessinsider.in, (May 11, 2022), https://www.businessinsider.in/international/news/a-black-texas-teen-was-suspended-from-school-and-told-he-couldnt-attend-graduation-due-to-the-length-of-his-hair/articleshow/91497948.cms.

[ccxxx] *Taylor Ardrey, A Black Texas teen was suspended from school and told he couldn't attend graduation due to the length of his hair*, businessinsider.in, (May 11, 2022), https://www.businessinsider.in/international/news/a-black-texas-teen-was-suspended-from-school-and-told-he-couldnt-attend-graduation-due-to-the-length-of-his-hair/articleshow/91497948.cms.

[ccxxxi] *Stacy Fernandez, ACLU warns 500 Texas school districts to revise discriminatory dress codes*, www.texastribune.org, (Sept. 4, 2020), https://www.texastribune.org/2020/09/04/texas-school-dress-code-aclu-hair-discrimination/.

[ccxxxii] *Stacy Fernandez, ACLU warns 500 Texas school districts to revise discriminatory dress codes*, www.texastribune.org, (Sept. 4, 2020), https://www.texastribune.org/2020/09/04/texas-school-dress-code-aclu-hair-discrimination/.

[ccxxxiii] *Michael Perchick, National governing body changes rule after Durham softball player forced to cut hair during game*, abc1.com, (July 14, 2021), https://abc11.com/nicole-pyles-hillside-high-national-federation-of-state-school-associations-nfhs/10887392/.

[ccxxxiv] The wearing of hair beads can be dated back to ancient history, most commonly see in hieroglyphics of ancient Egyptians. *See Damola Durosomo, Reclaiming Tradition: How Hair Beads Connect Us to Our History*, www.okayafrica.com, https://www.okayafrica.com/hair-beads-history-african-black-beauty-hair-jewelry-fulani-braids-twists-solange-floella-benjamin/ (last visited Aug. 20, 2022). Beads are commonly worn in the Black community and can have positive and negative connotations. *See generally id.*

[ccxxxv] *Michael Perchick, National governing body changes rule after Durham softball player forced to cut hair during game*, abc1.com, (July 14, 2021), https://abc11.com/nicole-pyles-hillside-high-national-federation-of-state-school-associations-nfhs/10887392/.

[ccxxxvi] *Michael Perchick, National governing body changes rule after Durham softball player forced to cut hair during game*, abc1.com, (July 14, 2021), https://abc11.com/nicole-pyles-hillside-high-national-federation-of-state-school-associations-nfhs/10887392/.

[ccxxxvii] *Michael Perchick, National governing body changes rule after Durham softball player forced to cut hair during game*, abc1.com, (July 14, 2021), https://abc11.com/nicole-pyles-hillside-high-national-federation-of-state-school-associations-nfhs/10887392/.

[ccxxxviii] *Michael Perchick, National governing body changes rule after Durham softball player forced to cut hair during game*, abc1.com, (July 14, 2021), https://abc11.com/nicole-pyles-hillside-high-national-federation-of-state-school-associations-nfhs/10887392/.

[ccxxxix] *Michael Perchick, National governing body changes rule after Durham softball player forced to cut hair during game*, abc1.com, (July 14, 2021), https://abc11.com/nicole-pyles-hillside-high-national-federation-of-state-school-associations-nfhs/10887392/.

[ccxl] *NFHS, Player Equipment Changes Highlight Rules Revisions in High School Softball*, www.nfhs.org, (July 12, 2021), https://www.nfhs.org/articles/player-equipment-changes-highlight-rules-revisions-in-high-school-softball/.

[ccxli] *NFHS, Player Equipment Changes Highlight Rules Revisions in High School Softball*, www.nfhs.org, (July 12, 2021), https://www.nfhs.org/articles/player-equipment-changes-highlight-rules-revisions-in-high-school-softball/.

[ccxlii] *NFHS, Player Equipment Changes Highlight Rules Revisions in High School Softball*, www.nfhs.org, (July 12, 2021), https://www.nfhs.org/articles/player-equipment-changes-highlight-rules-revisions-in-high-school-softball/.

[ccxliii] *Jenny Whidden, Legislation would bar school rules on hairstyles such as braids, cornrows that one mom says are rooted in 'respectability politics'*, chicagotribune.com, https://www.chicagotribune.com/coronavirus/ct-

[ccxliv] *Jenny Whidden, Legislation would bar school rules on hairstyles such as braids, cornrows that one mom says are rooted in 'respectability politics',* chicagotribune.com, https://www.chicagotribune.com/coronavirus/ct-illinois-hairstyle-discrimination-legislation-20210522-zg7ykipwmbgrze6i2e3nwnymou-story.html (May 21, 2021).

[ccxlv] *Jenny Whidden, Legislation would bar school rules on hairstyles such as braids, cornrows that one mom says are rooted in 'respectability politics',* chicagotribune.com, https://www.chicagotribune.com/coronavirus/ct-illinois-hairstyle-discrimination-legislation-20210522-zg7ykipwmbgrze6i2e3nwnymou-story.html (May 21, 2021).

[ccxlvi] *CBS Chicago, Gov. Pritzker Signs Jett Hawkins Act To Ban Discrimination Against Braids, Dreadlocks,* www.cbsnews.com, (Aug. 21, 2021), https://www.cbsnews.com/chicago/news/pritzker-jett-hawkins-act/; Jenny, Whidden, *Legislation would bar school rules on hairstyles such as braids, cornrows that one mom says are rooted in 'respectability politics',* chicagotribune.com, https://www.chicagotribune.com/coronavirus/ct-illinois-hairstyle-discrimination-legislation-20210522-zg7ykipwmbgrze6i2e3nwnymou-story.html (May 21, 2021).

[ccxlvii] Even though Providence St. Mel is a catholic school, the bill would include non-public schools. Illinois Federation of Teachers A Union of Professionals, *Resources to help schools implement the Jett Hawkins Law,* www.ift-aft.org, (Aug. 12, 2022), https://www.ift-aft.org/post/resources-to-help-schools-implement-the-jett-hawkins-law; Jenny, Whidden, *Legislation would bar school rules on hairstyles such as braids, cornrows that one mom says are rooted in 'respectability politics',* chicagotribune.com, https://www.chicagotribune.com/coronavirus/ct-illinois-hairstyle-discrimination-legislation-20210522-zg7ykipwmbgrze6i2e3nwnymou-story.html (May 21, 2021).

[ccxlviii] Illinois Federation of Teachers A Union of Professionals, *Resources to help schools implement the Jett Hawkins Law,* www.ift-aft.org, (Aug. 12, 2022), https://www.ift-aft.org/post/resources-to-help-schools-implement-the-jett-hawkins-law.

[ccxlix] Chris Bowling, A Nebraska school says it was a lice check. Lakota people sense centuries of repression, usatoday.com, https://www.usatoday.com/story/news/nation/2021/09/18/nebraska-lakota-culture-school-hair-cut-lice-check/8399799002/ (last updated Sept 20, 2021).

[ccl] Chris Bowling, A Nebraska school says it was a lice check. Lakota people sense centuries of repression, usatoday.com, https://www.usatoday.com/story/news/nation/2021/09/18/nebraska-lakota-culture-school-hair-cut-lice-check/8399799002/ (last updated Sept 20, 2021).

[ccli] Chris Bowling, A Nebraska school says it was a lice check. Lakota people sense centuries of repression, usatoday.com, https://www.usatoday.com/story/

[cclii] Chris Bowling, A Nebraska school says it was a lice check. Lakota people sense centuries of repression, usatoday.com, https://www.usatoday.com/story/news/nation/2021/09/18/nebraska-lakota-culture-school-hair-cut-lice-check/8399799002/ (last updated Sept 20, 2021).

[ccliii] Chris Bowling, A Nebraska school says it was a lice check. Lakota people sense centuries of repression, usatoday.com, https://www.usatoday.com/story/news/nation/2021/09/18/nebraska-lakota-culture-school-hair-cut-lice-check/8399799002/ (last updated Sept 20, 2021).

[ccliv] Chris Bowling, A Nebraska school says it was a lice check. Lakota people sense centuries of repression, usatoday.com, https://www.usatoday.com/story/news/nation/2021/09/18/nebraska-lakota-culture-school-hair-cut-lice-check/8399799002/ (last updated Sept 20, 2021).

[cclv] Chris Bowling, A Nebraska school says it was a lice check. Lakota people sense centuries of repression, usatoday.com, https://www.usatoday.com/story/news/nation/2021/09/18/nebraska-lakota-culture-school-hair-cut-lice-check/8399799002/ (last updated Sept 20, 2021).

[cclvi] Chris Bowling, A Nebraska school says it was a lice check. Lakota people sense centuries of repression, usatoday.com, https://www.usatoday.com/story/news/nation/2021/09/18/nebraska-lakota-culture-school-hair-cut-lice-check/8399799002/ (last updated Sept 20, 2021).

[cclvii] Chris Bowling, A Nebraska school says it was a lice check. Lakota people sense centuries of repression, usatoday.com, https://www.usatoday.com/story/news/nation/2021/09/18/nebraska-lakota-culture-school-hair-cut-lice-check/8399799002/ (last updated Sept 20, 2021).

[cclviii] Rayna Reid, *Minnesota Teacher Cuts Black Boy's Hair Without Permission*, www.essences.com, (Updated April 20, 2022), https://www.essence.com/news/teacher-cuts-boys-hair-without-permission/.

[cclix] Rayna Reid, *Minnesota Teacher Cuts Black Boy's Hair Without Permission*, www.essences.com, (Updated April 20, 2022), https://www.essence.com/news/teacher-cuts-boys-hair-without-permission/.

[cclx] Rayna Reid, *Minnesota Teacher Cuts Black Boy's Hair Without Permission*, www.essences.com, (Updated April 20, 2022), https://www.essence.com/news/teacher-cuts-boys-hair-without-permission/.

[cclxi] Gloria Oladipo, *Father sues Michigan school after teacher cuts daughter's hair without permission*, www.theguardian.com, (Sept. 20, 2021), https://www.theguardian.com/us-news/2021/sep/20/lawsuit-michigan-school-teacher-cut-girls-hair.

[cclxii] Gloria Oladipo, *Father sues Michigan school after teacher cuts daughter's hair without permission*, www.theguardian.com, (Sept. 20, 2021), https://www.theguardian.com/us-news/2021/sep/20/lawsuit-michigan-school-teacher-cut-girls-hair.

[cclxiii] Gloria Oladipo, *Father sues Michigan school after teacher cuts daughter's hair without permission*, www.theguardian.com, (Sept. 20, 2021), https://www.theguardian.com/us-news/2021/sep/20/lawsuit-michigan-school-teacher-cut-girls-hair.

[cclxiv] In California, a teach lost her job and faced criminal charges for allegedly forcing a student into a haircut while singing the national anthem. Kimberly Hutcherson, *California teacher faces charges after forcibly cutting a student's hair while singing anthem*, www.cnn.com, (Dec. 10, 2018), https://www.cnn.com/2018/12/08/us/california-haircut-teacher/index.html. This was a white student and a white teacher. *Id.* The same outrage that school officials displayed in this instance should be the same type of outrage that school officials have when it comes to Black hair discrimination. *Id.*

[cclxv] Iamlatrenda, Posted on March 11, 2022, Instagram, https://www.instagram.com/p/Ca-24wxOhrX/?igshid=YmMyMTA2M2Y= (last visited Apr. 13, 2022).

[cclxvi] Nia Rush, *Help Jacob be able to Walk across the stage for Graduation with his LOCS!*, change.org, https://www.change.org/p/grover-robinson-help-jacob-be-able-to-walk-across-the-stage-for-graduation-with-his-locs (last visited Apr. 13, 2022).

[cclxvii] Iamlatrenda, Posted on March 15, 2022, Instagram, https://www.instagram.com/p/CbIgErQOXxw/?igshid=YmMyMTA2M2Y= (last visited Apr. 13, 2022).

[cclxviii] Iamlatrenda, Posted on March 17, 2022, Instagram, https://www.instagram.com/p/CbN_N4auLgZ/?igshid=YmMyMTA2M2Y= (last visited Apr. 13, 2022).

[cclxix] Iamlatrenda, Posted on March 17, 2022, Instagram, https://www.instagram.com/p/CbN_N4auLgZ/?igshid=YmMyMTA2M2Y= (last visited Apr. 13, 2022).

[cclxx] Nia Rush, *Jacob Can Walk*, www.change.org, (Apr. 20, 2022), https://www.change.org/p/grover-robinson-help-jacob-be-able-to-walk-across-the-stage-for-graduation-with-his-locs/u/30463729?cs_tk=Arthv1534ODrRvKEaWIAAXicyyvNyQEABF8BvNlderB2-qYAwYpQVZDVpgQ%3D&utm_campaign=eb48ca16f21440ba92c19f8690abb3c9&utm_content=initial_v0_5_0&utm_medium=email&utm_source=petition_update&utm_term=cs

[cclxxi] the_nhsbc, Posted Apr. 6, 2022, Instagram, https://www.instagram.com/tv/CcADS87JhlA/?igshid=YmMyMTA2M2Y= (last visited Apr. 13, 2022); *Stephen Pimpo, Teen powerlifter forced to remove beads from hair*, www.wjtv.com, (Apr 20, 2022, Last updated Apr 20, 2022), https://www.wjtv.com/sports/the-sports-zone/teen-powerlifter-forced-to-remove-beads-from-hair/.

[cclxxii] the_nhsbc, Posted Apr. 6, 2022, Instagram, https://www.instagram.com/tv/CcADS87JhlA/?igshid=YmMyMTA2M2Y= (last visited

Apr. 13, 2022).

[cclxxiii] Stephen Pimpo, Teen powerlifter forced to remove beads from hair, www.wjtv.com, (Apr 20, 2022, Last updated Apr 20, 2022), https://www.wjtv.com/sports/the-sports-zone/teen-powerlifter-forced-to-remove-beads-from-hair/; The_nhsbc, Posted Apr. 6, 2022, Instagram, https://www.instagram.com/tv/CcADS87JhlA/?igshid=YmMyMTA2M2Y= (last visited Apr. 13, 2022).

[cclxxiv] Stephen Pimpo, Teen powerlifter forced to remove beads from hair, www.wjtv.com, (Apr 20, 2022, Last updated Apr 20, 2022), https://www.wjtv.com/sports/the-sports-zone/teen-powerlifter-forced-to-remove-beads-from-hair/; The_nhsbc, Posted Apr. 6, 2022, Instagram, https://www.instagram.com/tv/CcADS87JhlA/?igshid=YmMyMTA2M2Y= (last visited Apr. 13, 2022).

[cclxxv] Stephen Pimpo, Teen powerlifter forced to remove beads from hair, www.wjtv.com, (Apr 20, 2022, Last updated Apr 20, 2022), https://www.wjtv.com/sports/the-sports-zone/teen-powerlifter-forced-to-remove-beads-from-hair/.

[cclxxvi] *About Us*, bookings.edu, https://www.brookings.edu/about-us/(last visited Mar. 25, 2022); Jennifer Wyatt Bourgeois, *Penalizing Black hair in the name of academic success is undeniably racist, unfounded, and against the law*, (Feb. 23, 2021), bookings.edu, https://www.brookings.edu/blog/how-we-rise/2021/02/23/penalizing-black-hair-in-the-name-of-academic-success-is-undeniably-racist-unfounded-and-against-the-law/.

[cclxxvii] Jennifer Wyatt Bourgeois, *Penalizing Black hair in the name of academic success is undeniably racist, unfounded, and against the law*, (Feb. 23, 2021), bookings.edu, https://www.brookings.edu/blog/how-we-rise/2021/02/23/penalizing-black-hair-in-the-name-of-academic-success-is-undeniably-racist-unfounded-and-against-the-law/.

[cclxxviii] Jennifer Wyatt Bourgeois, *Penalizing Black hair in the name of academic success is undeniably racist, unfounded, and against the law*, (Feb. 23, 2021), bookings.edu, https://www.brookings.edu/blog/how-we-rise/2021/02/23/penalizing-black-hair-in-the-name-of-academic-success-is-undeniably-racist-unfounded-and-against-the-law/; Positive Behavioral Interventions and Support system is "an evidence-based three-tiered framework to improve and integrate all of the data, systems, and practices affecting student outcomes every day." The first tier "practices and systems establish a foundation of regular, proactive support while preventing unwanted behaviors. Schools provide these universal supports to all students, school-wide." *Id.* The second tier "practices and systems support students who are at risk for developing more serious problem behaviors before those behaviors start. . . [which] . . . help[s] students develop the skills they need to benefit from core programs at the school." *Id.* In the third tier "students receive more intensive, individualized support to improve their behavioral and academic outcomes. At this level, schools rely on formal assessments to determine a student's need." *Id.*

[cclxxix] *When Natural Hair Wins, Discrimination in School Loses*; nea.org, https://www.nea.org/advocating-for-change/new-from-nea/when-natural-hair-wins-discrimination-school-loses (last visited Sept. 15, 2021).

[cclxxx] About DREA, *Department of Racial Equity Advancement*, www.seattleschools.org, https://www.seattleschools.org/departments/drea/ (last visited Mar. 25, 2022).

[cclxxxi] Arielle Ingram-David, Senate Bill 174 signed at local Black-owned hair salon, www.alaskasnewssource.com, (Sept. 9, 2022), https://www.alaskasnewssource.com/2022/09/10/senate-bill-174-signed-local-black-owned-hair-salon/?outputType=amp&fbclid=IwAR0-Lgata8dFBZa9y6zB983sAmFXA6_u_Or0FLLVcp0w1hjfXg5olyzFbSs.

[cclxxxii] Arielle Ingram-David, Senate Bill 174 signed at local Black-owned hair salon, www.alaskasnewssource.com, (Sept. 9, 2022), https://www.alaskasnewssource.com/2022/09/10/senate-bill-174-signed-local-black-owned-hair-salon/?outputType=amp&fbclid=IwAR0-Lgata8dFBZa9y6zB983sAmFXA6_u_Or0FLLVcp0w1hjfXg5olyzFbSs.

[cclxxxiii] Arielle Ingram-David, Senate Bill 174 signed at local Black-owned hair salon, www.alaskasnewssource.com, (Sept. 9, 2022), https://www.alaskasnewssource.com/2022/09/10/senate-bill-174-signed-local-black-owned-hair-salon/?outputType=amp&fbclid=IwAR0-Lgata8dFBZa9y6zB983sAmFXA6_u_Or0FLLVcp0w1hjfXg5olyzFbSs.

[cclxxxiv] *When Natural Hair Wins, Discrimination in School Loses*; nea.org, https://www.nea.org/advocating-for-change/new-from-nea/when-natural-hair-wins-discrimination-school-loses (last visited Sept. 15, 2021); Mary Ellen Flannery, *Pushed Out: The Injustice Black Girls Face in School*, www.nea.org, (Sept 9. 2016), https://www.nea.org/advocating-for-change/new-from-nea/pushed-out-injustice-black-girls-face-school.

[cclxxxv] Jenna Fryer, *Ban on 'Soul Cap' spotlights lack of diversity in swimming*, apnews.com, (Aug. 1, 2021), https://apnews.com/article/2020-tokyo-olympics-swimming-soul-cap-ban-d6c88141801f7262f69eefbc05f0128a.

[cclxxxvi] *About*, Soul Cap, soulcap.com, https://soulcap.com/our-story.

[cclxxxvii] Jenna Fryer, *Ban on 'Soul Cap' spotlights lack of diversity in swimming*, apnews.com, (Aug. 1, 2021), https://apnews.com/article/2020-tokyo-olympics-swimming-soul-cap-ban-d6c88141801f7262f69eefbc05f0128a.

See Jenna Fryer, *Ban on 'Soul Cap' spotlights lack of diversity in swimming*, apnews.com, (Aug. 1, 2021), https://apnews.com/article/2020-tokyo-olympics-swimming-soul-cap-ban-d6c88141801f7262f69eefbc05f0128a.

[cclxxxviii] Christopher Luu, The Olympics Banned a Swim Cap for Afro Hair, instyle.com, (July 01, 2021), https://www.instyle.com/awards-events/sports/olympics/soul-cap-swim-cap-banned-tokyo-olympics; Edward Sutelan, *Olympic swim cap ban: What does 'Soul Cap' ruling mean for Black swimmers at 2021 Games?*, sportingnews.com, https://www.sportingnews.com/us/amp/

athletics/news/olympic-swim-cap-ban-2021-swimmers/3526wghlsb8v1ajeilz08cx41 (last visited Dec. 27, 2021).

[cclxxxix] *About FINA*, Overview, www.fina.org, https://www.fina.org/about (last visited Sept. 5, 2022); Jaclyn Diaz, *A swimming cap made for Black hair gets official approval after previous Olympic ban*, www.npr.org, (Sept. 2, 2022), https://www.npr.org/2022/09/02/1120761124/swimming-cap-black-hair-fina-approval.

[ccxc] Equality Act 2010, c. 15, https://www.legislation.gov.uk/ukpga/2010/15/contents
Rebekah Gougeon, Trowers & Hamlins, 'Black Hair' is Never 'Just Hair': A Closer Look at Afro Discrimination in the Workplace, law.com, (Oct. 28, 2021), https://www.law.com/international-edition/2021/10/28/black-hair-is-never-just-hair-a-closer-look-at-afro-discrimination-in-the-workplace/?slreturn=20211126112148.

[ccxci] *Rebekah Gougeon, Trowers & Hamlins, 'Black Hair' is Never 'Just Hair': A Closer Look at Afro Discrimination in the Workplace*, law.com, (Oct. 28, 2021), https://www.law.com/international-edition/2021/10/28/black-hair-is-never-just-hair-a-closer-look-at-afro-discrimination-in-the-workplace/?slreturn=20211126112148.

[ccxcii] *See* Rogers v. Am. Airlines, Inc., 527 F. Supp. 229, 232 (S.D.N.Y. 1981).

[ccxciii] *Shamaan Freeman-Powell, Hair discrimination should be designated as a form of racism, campaigners and MPs say*, news.sky.com, (Oct. 20, 2021), https://news.sky.com/story/amp/hair-discrimination-should-be-designated-as-a-form-of-racism-campaigners-and-mps-say-12438867.

[ccxciv] *Halo Code: What is is and how does it protect afro hair?*, www.bbc.com, (Dec. 10, 2020), https://www.bbc.com/newsround/55249674; *Fiona Embleton, Halo Code: The UK's first Afro hair code has launched to end discrimination*, www.womanandhome.com, (Dec. 10, 2020), https://www.womanandhome.com/us/beauty/beauty-news/halo-code-afro-hair-discrimination/.

[ccxcv] *Halo Code: What is is and how does it protect afro hair?*, www.bbc.com, (Dec. 10, 2020), https://www.bbc.com/newsround/55249674 ; *Fiona Embleton, Halo Code: The UK's first Afro hair code has launched to end discrimination*, www.womanandhome.com, (Dec. 10, 2020), https://www.womanandhome.com/us/beauty/beauty-news/halo-code-afro-hair-discrimination/.

[ccxcvi] *Fiona Embleton, Halo Code: The UK's first Afro hair code has launched to end discrimination*, www.womanandhome.com, (Dec. 10, 2020), https://www.womanandhome.com/beauty/beauty-news/halo-code-afro-hair-discrimination/; *The CROWN Act*, www.dove.com, https://www.dove.com/us/en/stories/campaigns/the-crown-act.html (last visited Sept. 24, 2022).

[ccxcvii] *Michelle De Leon and Denese Chikwendu, World Afro Day: Hair Equality*

[ccxcviii] *Michelle De Leon and Denese Chikwendu, World Afro Day: Hair Equality Report 2019*, https://static1.squarespace.com/static/58c1d7399f7456c9116ad8c8/t/5cd352044785d3e44d72abef/1557352966574/WAD+Hair+Equality+Report+2019.pdf (last visited Mar. 24, 2022).

[ccxcix] *Michelle De Leon and Denese Chikwendu, World Afro Day: Hair Equality Report 2019*, https://static1.squarespace.com/static/58c1d7399f7456c9116ad8c8/t/5cd352044785d3e44d72abef/1557352966574/WAD+Hair+Equality+Report+2019.pdf (last visited Mar. 24, 2022).

[ccc] *Michelle De Leon and Denese Chikwendu, World Afro Day: Hair Equality Report 2019*, https://static1.squarespace.com/static/58c1d7399f7456c9116ad8c8/t/5cd352044785d3e44d72abef/1557352966574/WAD+Hair+Equality+Report+2019.pdf (last visited Mar. 24, 2022).

[ccci] *Michelle De Leon and Denese Chikwendu, World Afro Day: Hair Equality Report 2019*, https://static1.squarespace.com/static/58c1d7399f7456c9116ad8c8/t/5cd352044785d3e44d72abef/1557352966574/WAD+Hair+Equality+Report+2019.pdf (last visited Mar. 24, 2022).

[cccii] *Michelle De Leon and Denese Chikwendu, World Afro Day: Hair Equality Report 2019*, https://static1.squarespace.com/static/58c1d7399f7456c9116ad8c8/t/5cd352044785d3e44d72abef/1557352966574/WAD+Hair+Equality+Report+2019.pdf (last visited Mar. 24, 2022).

[ccciii] *Michelle De Leon and Denese Chikwendu, World Afro Day: Hair Equality Report 2019*, https://static1.squarespace.com/static/58c1d7399f7456c9116ad8c8/t/5cd352044785d3e44d72abef/1557352966574/WAD+Hair+Equality+Report+2019.pdf (last visited Mar. 24, 2022).

[ccciv] *Michelle De Leon and Denese Chikwendu, World Afro Day: Hair Equality Report 2019*, https://static1.squarespace.com/static/58c1d7399f7456c9116ad8c8/t/5cd352044785d3e44d72abef/1557352966574/WAD+Hair+Equality+Report+2019.pdf (last visited Mar. 24, 2022).

[cccv] *Michelle De Leon and Denese Chikwendu, World Afro Day: Hair Equality Report 2019*, https://static1.squarespace.com/static/58c1d7399f7456c9116ad8c8/t/5cd352044785d3e44d72abef/1557352966574/WAD+Hair+Equality+Report+2019.pdf (last visited Mar. 24, 2022).

[cccvi] *Michelle De Leon and Denese Chikwendu, World Afro Day: Hair Equality Report 2019*, https://static1.squarespace.com/static/58c1d7399f7456c9116ad8c8/

[cccvii] *Michelle De Leon and Denese Chikwendu, World Afro Day: Hair Equality Report 2019*, https://static1.squarespace.com/static/58c1d7399f7456c9116ad8c8/t/5cd352044785d3e44d72abef/1557352966574/WAD+Hair+Equality+Report+2019.pdf (last visited Mar. 24, 2022).

[cccviii] *Michelle De Leon and Denese Chikwendu, World Afro Day: Hair Equality Report 2019*, https://static1.squarespace.com/static/58c1d7399f7456c9116ad8c8/t/5cd352044785d3e44d72abef/1557352966574/WAD+Hair+Equality+Report+2019.pdf (last visited Mar. 24, 2022).

[cccix] *See Michelle De Leon and Denese Chikwendu, World Afro Day: Hair Equality Report 2019*, https://static1.squarespace.com/static/58c1d7399f7456c9116ad8c8/t/5cd352044785d3e44d72abef/1557352966574/WAD+Hair+Equality+Report+2019.pdf (last visited Mar. 24, 2022).

[cccx] Civil Rights Act of 1964, 42 U.S.C. § 2000e et seq (1964), *See Michelle De Leon and Denese Chikwendu, World Afro Day: Hair Equality Report 2019*, https://static1.squarespace.com/static/58c1d7399f7456c9116ad8c8/t/5cd352044785d3e44d72abef/1557352966574/WAD+Hair+Equality+Report+2019.pdf (last visited Mar. 24, 2022).

[cccxi] *See Michelle De Leon and Denese Chikwendu, World Afro Day: Hair Equality Report 2019*, https://static1.squarespace.com/static/58c1d7399f7456c9116ad8c8/t/5cd352044785d3e44d72abef/1557352966574/WAD+Hair+Equality+Report+2019.pdf (last visited Mar. 24, 2022).

[cccxii] *See Michelle De Leon and Denese Chikwendu, World Afro Day: Hair Equality Report 2019*, https://static1.squarespace.com/static/58c1d7399f7456c9116ad8c8/t/5cd352044785d3e44d72abef/1557352966574/WAD+Hair+Equality+Report+2019.pdf (last visited Mar. 24, 2022).

[cccxiii] *Emma Dabiri, Black pupils are being wrongly excluded over their hair. I'm trying to end this discrimination*, www.theguardian.com, (Feb. 25, 2022), https://www.theguardian.com/commentisfree/2020/feb/25/black-pupils-excluded-hair-discrimination-equality-act.

[cccxiv] *Emma Dabiri, Black pupils are being wrongly excluded over their hair. I'm trying to end this discrimination*, www.theguardian.com, (Feb. 25, 2022), https://www.theguardian.com/commentisfree/2020/feb/25/black-pupils-excluded-hair-discrimination-equality-act.

[cccxv] *Emma Dabiri, Black pupils are being wrongly excluded over their hair. I'm trying to end this discrimination*, www.theguardian.com, (Feb. 25, 2022), https://www.theguardian.com/commentisfree/2020/feb/25/black-

pupils-excluded-hair-discrimination-equality-act.

[cccxvi] *Emma Dabiri, Black pupils are being wrongly excluded over their hair. I'm trying to end this discrimination,* www.theguardian.com, (Feb. 25, 2022), https://www.theguardian.com/commentisfree/2020/feb/25/black-pupils-excluded-hair-discrimination-equality-act.

[cccxvii] *Halo, A Short History Of Hair Discrimination,* **halocollective.co.uk**, https://halocollective.co.uk/halo-background/ (last visited Mar 24, 2022).

[cccxviii] Kameron Virk, *Ruby Williams: No Child with afro hair should suffer like me,* www.bbc.com, (Feb. 10, 2020), https://www.bbc.com/news/newsbeat-45521094.amp.

[cccxix] Kameron Virk, *Ruby Williams: No Child with afro hair should suffer like me,* www.bbc.com, (Feb. 10, 2020), https://www.bbc.com/news/newsbeat-45521094.amp.

[cccxx] *Jada Jackson, Some South African Schools Still Have "Blatantly Racist" Dress Codes,* (Nov. 2, 2021), www.allure.com, https://www.allure.com/story/zulaikha-patel-hair-discrimination-interview; *Koketso Moeti, Stop Racism at Pretoria Girls High,* awethu.amandla.mobi/, https://awethu.amandla.mobi/petitions/stop-racism-at-pretoria-girls-high (last visited Mar. 25, 2022).

[cccxxi] *Thabile Vilakazi, South African students protest against school's alleged racist hair policy,* www.cnn.com, (Sept. 1, 2016), https://www.cnn.com/2016/08/31/africa/south-africa-school-racism/index.html.

[cccxxii] *Luso Mnthali, Anti-Blackness At Its Core: Pretoria Girls High School Protests Are About More Than Hair,* www.essence.com, (Updated Oct. 26, 2020), https://www.essence.com/news/pretoria-racist-hair-rule-protests/.

[cccxxiii] *Luso Mnthali, Anti-Blackness At Its Core: Pretoria Girls High School Protests Are About More Than Hair,* www.essence.com, (Updated Oct. 26, 2020), https://www.essence.com/news/pretoria-racist-hair-rule-protests.

[cccxxiv] *Jada Jackson, Some South African Schools Still Have "Blatantly Racist" Dress Codes,* (Nov. 2, 2021), www.allure.com, https://www.allure.com/story/zulaikha-patel-hair-discrimination-interview.

[cccxxv] The students are in what America would call grade 10 and 11. *Caitlin Cassidy, Sisters of African descent suspended from Victorian private school for not tying hair back,* www.theguardian.com, (July 29, 2022), https://www.theguardian.com/australia-news/2022/jul/29/sisters-suspended-from-victorian-private-school-highview-college-maryborough-for-refusing-to-wear-their-african-hair-tied-back.

[cccxxvi] *Caitlin Cassidy, Sisters of African descent suspended from Victorian private school for not tying hair back,* www.theguardian.com, (July 29, 2022), https://www.theguardian.com/australia-news/2022/jul/29/sisters-suspended-from-victorian-private-school-highview-college-maryborough-for-refusing-to-wear-their-african-hair-tied-back.

[cccxxvii] *See Caitlin Cassidy, Sisters of African descent suspended from Victorian private school for not tying hair back,* www.theguardian.com, (July 29, 2022), https://www.theguardian.com/australia-news/2022/jul/29/sisters-suspended-from-victorian-private-school-highview-college-maryborough-for-refusing-to-wear-their-african-hair-tied-back.

[cccxxviii] *Caitlin Cassidy, Sisters of African descent suspended from Victorian private school for not tying hair back*, www.theguardian.com, (July 29, 2022), https://www.theguardian.com/australia-news/2022/jul/29/sisters-suspended-from-victorian-private-school-highview-college-maryborough-for-refusing-to-wear-their-african-hair-tied-back.

[cccxxix] *Caitlin Cassidy, Sisters of African descent suspended from Victorian private school for not tying hair back*, www.theguardian.com, (July 29, 2022), https://www.theguardian.com/australia-news/2022/jul/29/sisters-suspended-from-victorian-private-school-highview-college-maryborough-for-refusing-to-wear-their-african-hair-tied-back.

[cccxxx] *Caitlin Cassidy, Sisters of African descent suspended from Victorian private school for not tying hair back*, www.theguardian.com, (July 29, 2022), https://www.theguardian.com/australia-news/2022/jul/29/sisters-suspended-from-victorian-private-school-highview-college-maryborough-for-refusing-to-wear-their-african-hair-tied-back.

[cccxxxi] *Halo, A Short History Of Hair Discrimination*, **halocollective.co.uk**, https://halocollective.co.uk/halo-background/ (last Mar 24, 2022).

[cccxxxii] *Halo, A Short History Of Hair Discrimination*, **halocollective.co.uk**, https://halocollective.co.uk/halo-background/ (last Mar 24, 2022); *April Maria Williams*, My Hair Is Professional TOO!, (2020).

[cccxxxiii] *Halo, A Short History Of Hair Discrimination*, **halocollective.co.uk**, https://halocollective.co.uk/halo-background/ (last visited Mar 24, 2022).

[cccxxxiv] *Halo, A Short History Of Hair Discrimination*, **halocollective.co.uk**, https://halocollective.co.uk/halo-background/ (last visited Mar 24, 2022).

[cccxxxv] Adele Norris, Hair Discrimination and Global Politics of Anti-Blackness, Part 1, WWW.AAIHS.ORG, (Oct. 19, 2021), https://www.aaihs.org/hair-discrimination-and-global-politics-of-anti-blackness-part-1/.

[cccxxxvi] *Hair Love*, Main, www.matthewacherry.com, http://www.matthewacherry.com/hair-love (last visited Feb. 18, 2022).

[cccxxxvii] *Hair Love*, imdb.com, https://www.imdb.com/title/tt7129636/ (last visited Feb 18, 2022).

[cccxxxviii] Karma's World, Hair Comes Trouble, Netflix, Oct. 15, 2021.

[cccxxxix] Karma's World, Hair Comes Trouble, Netflix, Oct. 15, 2021.

[cccxl] Karma's World, Hair Comes Trouble, Netflix, Oct. 15, 2021.

[cccxli] Rise Up and Sing Out, Super Bonnet, Disney, Feb. 2, 2022.

[cccxlii] Rise Up and Sing Out, Super Bonnet, Disney, Feb. 2, 2022.

[cccxliii] Tony Abari, 52 Black Kids Shows You Can Watch Right Now, www.matermea.com, https://matermea.com/52-black-kids-tv-shows-you-can-watch-right-now/ (last visited Feb. 22, 2022) [cccxliv] Gracie's Corner, youtube.com, https://www.youtube.com/channel/UCQ2FzqlvWSE7ysvL1sLWQ5Q (last visited Feb. 25, 2022).

[cccxlv] Gracie's Corner, I Love My Hair, youtube.com, (Aug. 28, 2020), https://www.youtube.com/watch?v=AXrLePgwO4c (last visited Feb. 25, 2022).

[cccxlvi] Matthew A. Cherry, Hair Love, (2019).

[cccxlvii] *NoNieqa Ramos*, Hair Story, (2021).

[cccxlviii] Colleen Dixon, Coco Love Her Curly Hair, (2020).

[cccxlix] *Rashawn Ray and Alexandra Gibbons, Why are states banning critical race theory?*, brookings.com, (Nov. 2021), https://www.brookings.edu/blog/fixgov/2021/07/02/why-are-states-banning-critical-race-theory/.

[cccl] *Rashawn Ray and Alexandra Gibbons, Why are states banning critical race theory?*, brookings.com, (Nov. 2021), https://www.brookings.edu/blog/fixgov/2021/07/02/why-are-states-banning-critical-race-theory/.

[cccli] Zack Tawatari, *Author's books pulled from Katy ISD shelves, speaking engagement postponed over critical race theory concerns*, www.khou.com, (Oct. 11, 2021), https://www.khou.com/article/news/education/jerry-craft-books-critical-race-theory-concerns-katy-isd/285-2932b642-7694-4349-9a8a-b650fcfe26e8.

[ccclii] Zack Tawatari, *Author's books pulled from Katy ISD shelves, speaking engagement postponed over critical race theory concerns*, www.khou.com, (Oct. 11, 2021), https://www.khou.com/article/news/education/jerry-craft-books-critical-race-theory-concerns-katy-isd/285-2932b642-7694-4349-9a8a-b650fcfe26e8.

[cccliii] Bruce C.T. Wright, *Little League Baseball Denies Racism After White Teammates Cover Black Player's Hair With Cotton*, newsone.com, (Aug. 23, 2022), https://newsone.com/4395302/little-league-cotton-controversy/; TMZ Sports, *Little League World Series Black Player Covered In Cotton... Officials Say 'No Ill-Intent' Behind Actions*, www.tmz.com, (Aug. 22, 2022), https://www.tmz.com/2022/08/22/little-league-world-series-no-ill-intent-cotton-player-head/.

[cccliv] *Natasha Marsh, Molly's Big Chop on This Season of Insecure Is a Love Letter to Working Black Women Everywhere*, popsugar.com.au, https://www.popsugar.com.au/beauty/molly-twa-haircut-insecure-season-5-meaning-48595535/amp (last visited Jan. 14, 2022).

[ccclv] Insure, HBO, Oct. 9, 2016.

[ccclvi] Our Kind Of People, Sept. 21, 2021.

[ccclvii] Bad Hair, Hulu Neon, Jan. 23, 2020.

[ccclviii] Bad Hair, Hulu Neon, Jan. 23, 2020.

[ccclix] Bad Hair, Hulu Neon, Jan. 23, 2020.

[ccclx] April Maria Williams, Esq., My Hair Is Professional TOO!, Jumptime Publishing (2020).

[ccclxi] April Maria Williams, Esq., My Hair Is Professional TOO!, (2020).

[ccclxii] Jenny R. Yang and Jane Liu, *Strengthening accountability for discrimination*, (Jan. 19, 2021), www.epi.org, https://www.epi.org/unequalpower/publications/strengthening-accountability-for-discrimination-confronting-fundamental-power-imbalances-in-the-employment-relationship/.

[ccclxiii] Jenny R. Yang and Jane Liu, *Strengthening accountability for discrimination*, (Jan. 19, 2021), www.epi.org, https://www.epi.org/unequalpower/publications/strengthening-accountability-for-discrimination-confronting-fundamental-power-imbalances-in-the-employment-relationship/.

[ccclxiv] Jenny R. Yang and Jane Liu, *Strengthening accountability for discrimination*, (Jan. 19, 2021), www.epi.org, https://www.epi.org/unequalpower/publications/strengthening-accountability-for-discrimination-confronting-fundamental-power-imbalances-in-the-employment-relationship/.

[ccclxv] *Nurse Blake*, NO MORE MESSY BUNS?!?!, (July 28, 2022), https://www.facebook.com/photo/?fbid=609784750503631&set=a.287904279358348.

[ccclxvi] See post comments. *Nurse Blake*, NO MORE MESSY BUNS?!?!, (July 28, 2022), https://www.facebook.com/photo/?fbid=609784750503631&set=a.287904279358348.

[ccclxvii] *See African Studies Center – University Of Pennsylvania*, "Letter from a Birmingham Jail [King, Jr.]", www.africa.upenn.edu, https://www.africa.upenn.edu/Articles_Gen/Letter_Birmingham.html (Last visited May 30, 2022).

[ccclxviii] Alli Fam, *Shifting the Black hair care industry back into Black hands*, marketplace.org, July 28, 202, https://www.marketplace.org/2020/07/28/shifting-black-hair-care-industry-back-into-black-hands/.

[ccclxix] *Tayo Bero, Black women's hair products are killing. Why isn't more being done*, theguardian.com, July 27, 2021, ushttps://www.theguardian.com/commentisfree/2021/jul/27/black-women-hair-products-health-hazards-study

[ccclxx] Eric Jensen, et. al., *The Chance That Two People Chosen at Random Are of Different Race or Ethnicity Groups Has Increased Since 2010*, www.census.gov, (Aug. 12, 2021), https://www.census.gov/library/stories/2021/08/2020-united-states-population-more-racially-ethnically-diverse-than-2010.html.

MY HAIR IS STILL PROFESSIONAL TOO!: WHERE ARE WE NOW?

www.ingramcontent.com/pod-product-compliance
Lightning Source LLC
Chambersburg PA
CBHW021915180426
43198CB00035B/671